Transport Disadvantage and Social Exclusion

Exclusionary Mechanisms in Transport in Urban Scotland

JULIAN HINE
Transport and Road Assessment Centre, University of Ulster, UK
FIONA MITCHELL
University of York, UK

ASHGATE

Published by
Ashgate Publishing Limited
Gower House
Croft Road
Aldershot
Hants GU11 3HR
England

Ashgate Publishing Company
Suite 420
101 Cherry Street
Burlington, VT 05401-4405
USA

Ashgate website: http://www.ashgate.com

British Library Cataloguing in Publication Data
Hine, Julian
    Transport disadvantage and social exclusion : exclusion
    mechanisms in transport in urban Scotland. - (Transport and
    society)
    1. Transportation - Social aspects - Scotland 2. Marginality,
    Social - Scotland 3. Transportation and state - Scotland
    I. Title II. Mitchell, Fiona
    303.4'832'09411

Library of Congress Cataloging-in-Publication Data
Hine, Julian.
    Transport disadvantage and social exclusion : exclusion mechanisms in transport in
urban Scotland / Julian Hine and Fiona Mitchell.
        p. cm. -- (Transport and society)
    Includes bibliographical references.
    ISBN 0-7546-1847-1 (alk. paper)
    1. Urban transportation--Scotland. 2. Social isolation--Scotland. I. Mitchell, Fiona. II.
Title. III. Series.

HE311.S35 T73 2003
388.4'09411--dc21

2002190867

ISBN 0 7546 1847 1

Printed and bound in Great Britain by
Antony Rowe Ltd., Chippenham, Wiltshire

Contents

List of Figures

List of Tables

Acknowledgements

This book has taken a great deal of time to put together. Indeed more than I thought it would. The book is based on work that Fiona and myself undertook for the Scottish Executive some time ago. I would like to take this opportunity to recognise the support that they gave us when undertaking this work for them. I would also like to thank the University of Ulster, who gave me the time and space to complete this volume. Lastly I would like to thank my wife, Elaine, and family for their support during this time.

Julian Hine
University of Ulster

Chapter 1

A Forgotten Transport Problem?

Introduction

The link between transport and social exclusion has until recently been widely ignored by policy makers and governments. The importance of this link has been highlighted by a number of recent studies (DETR, 2000a; Hine and Mitchell, 2001a; Church et al., 2000; Lucas et al., 2001). The traditional concern of transport policy makers with car dependence and the journey to work has inevitably resulted in a policy focus that by its very nature ignores poverty and the consequences of non-car ownership in terms of access to new employment centres, retail facilities (now invariably located at out of town or peripheral locations) and educational facilities. In the mid- and late 1990s it was possible to state that, although the existence of a link between transport and social exclusion had been widely recognised, it could also be concluded that there was a lack of clear and reliable data (Barry, 1998; Pacione, 1995). As recently as 1999 it was concluded in a study of transport and social exclusion in London that the paucity of data on the issue meant that the relationship between transport and social exclusion could not be fully appreciated (Church et al., 1999, 2000).

Social exclusion reflects the existence of these barriers which make it difficult or impossible for people to participate fully in society (Social Exclusion Unit, 1998). Studies have identified a number of factors that are seen to contribute to social exclusion, including differentials in education and training opportunity and attainment, socioeconomic circumstances, local environment, peer group, as well as access to information and physical accessibility to a wide range of opportunities including employment, shopping and recreation. Access to an adequate transport system is central to all of these.

In the UK the focus of the debate has been concerned with the gap between poor neighbourhoods and the 'rest' where social and economic changes have resulted in mass joblessness, as a consequence of the decline of manufacturing industry and the need for new skills; concentration of vulnerable people in deprived neighbourhoods; family breakdown; poor core public services and public service failure; declining popularity of social housing. The problem in these areas has been compounded by a lack of attention to links between poor neighbourhoods and local and regional economies, and poor links between planning and economic development which can accentuate the barriers to work, education and child care (Social Exclusion Unit, 2001; Hine and Mitchell, 2001a).

UK transport policy is now seeking to address the transport-related dimensions of social exclusion. The recent UK Transport White Paper produced in 1998 stated transport helps to make a 'fairer society' (DETR, 1998a, p. 9). This has placed a new importance and urgency on identifying the nature of the linkage between transport disadvantage and social exclusion, and the mechanisms by which an integrated transport system can reduce levels of exclusion. In the UK this debate about transport and social exclusion has been accorded a lower priority at a time when a series of new interventions in the local transport market have been proposed and incorporated in new Transport Acts for England and Wales, and Scotland. It can be argued that these interventions that include the development of Quality Partnerships, Quality Contracts and charging mechanisms such as road pricing and the Work Place Parking Levy are essentially targeted at modal shift from private car to public transport and the encouragement of more environmentally friendly modes of transport such as walking and cycling. This issue will be discussed in more detail later in this volume. The paradox here is that in communities where walking accounts for a significant proportion of trips public transport is seen to be ineffective and a failure by users. In these areas, which are important markets for public transport providers in terms of their market share, car access is shared with family and friends.

Increasingly poorer communities can lose services due to the restructuring of bus routes into areas of new employment and those housing areas where those live who possess the new skills vital for the new service economy. The irony is that it is these areas where car ownership is relatively higher and rising. The modal shift argument favoured by policy makers is credible for these areas but not for those urban areas where car ownership is low and deprivation high. For rural areas similar arguments have been made. Evidence from Scotland, the northeast of England, London and New Deal areas in the DETR study highlight this problem (Hine and Mitchell, 2001a; DETR, 2001; www.goneat.org.uk; Farrington et al., 1998).

Central to this volume are a number of key questions that relate to the direction of UK transport policy (that is what transport policy currently is and also what it can become), its delivery and the very nature of social exclusion. These are:

- how is the link between transport and social exclusion characterised;
- given this characterisation, what policy mechanisms and practices are appropriate in different circumstances;
- what are the implications of the social exclusion debate for the delivery and organisation of transport policy?

Forgotten Problem?

The process of social exclusion and the relationship with transport is little understood by local authorities, and it is these authorities who regularly intervene in the local transport market to subsidise public transport services that are socially necessary (Sinclair et al., 2001; Hine and Mitchell, 2001a). Exclusion is about non-participation of individuals across a range of life shaping activities including employment, education and leisure. A number of authors (Burchardt et al., 1999; Lee and Murie, 1999; Church et al., 2001) have identified dimensional frameworks to illustrate the problem and also focus research activity (discussed later in this chapter). From a transport viewpoint, access and mobility are key to all these activities. It is access to transport – or, in many cases, the lack of it – that shapes lives and confines certain groups in certain locations to particular labour markets and opportunities. Due to historical patterns of investment in the transport system and land use planning decisions, these activities may now increasingly be further away, for reasons associated with economies of scale, and as a consequence located at points not well served by public transport and readily accessible by private car.

Scatters and Clusters

Other issues arise for the policy maker when deciding how to deal with social excluded groups in terms of delivering transport and other goods and services. This is the small matter of 'scatters' and 'clusters' (Grieco, Turner and Hine, 2000). Socially excluded groups are not only found clustered in particular areas; they can also be found in scatters as a consequence of life circumstance. For example, older people living in many affluent urban and suburban areas provide an example of a scatter. This represents a fundamentally different problem for policy makers than a cluster does. It has been argued that, indeed, the scatter of socially excluded individuals and households can be better served through new information technologies. In the recent Scottish Executive study of transport and social inclusion (Hine and Mitchell, 2001a), 40 per cent of households were found to have a PC. The next step of access to information technology via this route may not be far away in lower income areas. It is access to information via either a PC or telephone that may mitigate against poor and infrequent transport services and even allow community transport or other transport providers to provide services such as taxis, that are a bookable resource. The problem here may be that, for commercial operators, such services are not viable and, for local authorities, they may involve a substantial reshaping of spending patterns on local authority transport. A common problem within local authorities is the difficulty of negotiating shared transport schemes between different local authority departments, for example between education and social services.

For clusters of the socially excluded it may be relatively easier to provide services and they may offer a better fit with existing bus routes and schedules. That is not say to that clusters are not without their problems. In circumstances where subsidised services are offered at particular times of the day to help people access job opportunities in other areas, the services may be well used initially but then operators experience a decline in patronage as these passengers become more established in the work force and begin to be able to share transport with colleagues or even, over a period of time, purchase a car. The problem of the transient cluster in transport terms needs to be recognised and more thought is required to deal with this problem, as it can affect the viability of a whole route in the long run. Service withdrawal and the alignment of services on profitable corridors is not unheard off and there are plenty of examples around the UK.

A New Policy?

As highlighted earlier at the start of this chapter, a fear is that current policy as enshrined in the new Transport Acts for England, Wales and Scotland will be more effective in dealing with the modal shift question rather than poverty reduction and creating transport opportunities for socially excluded groups. It is clear that the legislation provides transport authorities with policy tools that could be responsible for creating effective public transport systems and encourage modal shift, but they may also inadvertently promote a realignment of public transport services on corridors away from and towards the edge of areas where socially excluded groups reside.

New public transport markets are deemed to exist among the wealthier car commuter households, who favour more frequent services that are quicker and more direct. In planning routes operators must also strike a balance with their core business amongst their regular users who have lower levels of access to the private car. To protect their business, public transport operators will reshape their networks to meet the needs of changing local economies. The skills and qualifications demanded by these new local economies are such that excluded groups may be increasingly marginalised unless transport services or arrangements can be found that can allow access to areas where new opportunities exist. These market trends, aimed at the car commuter, could work against those in lower income areas who do not own cars and who rely on public transport to get them to work. Those who rely on their local bus network could very well find that it will take longer, operate less frequently and not fit with the new patterns (shift work) or the location of their employment. Instead, bus-based public transport services will be concentrated on quality partnership routes that guarantee a larger market share and afford the operator the opporunity to run services at a greater frequency for longer periods during the day. The concern arises where communities and particular user groups are located considerable distances from these main corridors which are being made increasingly important by state intervention in partnership with public transport operators. The realisation that local public transport links are vital to the sustainability of communities has recently been recognised by central government with the extension of the Bus Challenge Scheme to urban areas over the period 2001 to 2004 (Social Exclusion Unit, 2001; DLTR, 2001).

How can Social Exclusion be Conceptualised?

The debate about social exclusion has origins in earlier debates in the literature on poverty, deprivation and the underclass. Social exclusion has come to be accepted as a term that refers to the loss of 'ability (by people or households) to both literally and metaphorically connect with many of the jobs, services and facilities that they need to participate fully in society' (Church and Frost, 1999, p. 3). Poverty and deprivation, on the other hand, refer to a lack of access to material welfare, and material and social deprivation (Folwell, 1999). In a transport policy and land use planning setting the notion of exclusion as an explanation has certain attractions; it is a process whereby households and individuals experience a progressive isolation or lack of connectivity to jobs, goods and services. This process results in a deterioration in participation across a number of areas (Church et al., 1999; McCormick and Leicester, 1998; De Haan, 1999).

In transport terms the argument can be made that a lack of access to effective transport can impact on the extent to which individuals can access health facilities, local job markets and leisure activities. According to Gaffron, Hine and Mitchell (2001) there is broad agreement in the literature that social exclusion represents a conceptual shift away from the traditional forms of explanation and should not be considered equivalent to older terms and definitions previously applied to individuals, groups and processes considered to exist and operate outside a certain social norm – such as poverty, deprivation and the underclass (Bhalla and Lapeyre, 1997; Lee and Murie, 1999). It is enough at this point, and for our purposes in this volume, to note this. In transport terms the links between poverty and transport disadvantage have been known for some time: social exclusion provides an added dimension in terms of the process and dynamic. It also raises a number of questions about policy delivery, as we have seen in relation to the earlier discussion about scatters and clusters.

Despite there being no common definition of social exclusion, there was also found to be no common definition of the dimensions and factors involved in it. But in both cases, the approaches taken by various authors, though different in detail, broadly overlap (Gaffron, Hine and Mitchell, 2001). Lee and Murie (1999) identified eight areas under which social exclusion could be discussed and examined. These were: labour markets and employment; welfare markets and poverty traps; exclusion from financial circuits and public utilities; education; health; housing markets; neighbourhoods and social networks. In another study Burchardt et al. (1999) developed a dimensional framework to identify not only areas and activities that social exclusion could impact upon but also how the effect of exclusion could potentially be measured across these areas of activities. This framework included:

- consumption activity – the ability to consume at least to a certain level the goods and services considered normal for the society;
- savings activity – the ability to accumulate savings and pension entitlements and/or to own property, both as way of fulfilling individual and social aspirations (such as home ownership) and to provide security for periods outside the labour market;
- production activity – the ability to engage in an economically and/or socially valued activity (including paid work, education, training, retirement over state pension age or looking after a family), which helps the individual to gain or maintain self-respect for being engaged in an activity valued by others and makes a direct or indirect economic contribution to society;

- political activity – the ability to engage in some collective effort to improve or protect the immediate or wider social and physical environment (including voting, membership of political parties and or campaigning groups);
- social activity – the ability to engage in significant social interaction with family or friends and identifying with a cultural group or community (social isolation and denial of cultural rights are considered significant factors in social exclusion).

Burchardt et al. also recognised that the ability of a group or individual to participate across these dimensions could be affected by a number of factors. These include the individual's own characteristics, life events, characteristics of the area resided in and social, civil and political institutions of society. Church et al. (1999, 2000) identified categories of exclusion that are connected to transport and proposed three types of processes that influence this relationship between exclusion and transport. They were: 1) the nature of time-space organisation in households; 2) the nature of the transport system; and 3) the nature of time/space organisation of the facilities and opportunities individuals are seeking to access. The nature of these will differ according to gender, age, cultural background, level of ability and economic circumstances. The seven categories of exclusion connected to transport suggested by Church et al. are:

- *physical exclusion* – where physical barriers inhibit the accessibility of services, which could be experienced by mothers with children, elderly or frail, those encumbered by heavy loads or those who do not speak the dominant language of the society;
- *geographical exclusion* – where poor transport provision and resulting inaccessibility can create exclusion not just in rural areas but also in areas on the urban fringe;
- *exclusion from facilities* – the distance of facilities – e.g. shopping, health, leisure, education – from people's homes, especially from those with no car, making access difficult;
- *economic exclusion* – the high monetary or temporal costs of travel can prevent or limit access to facilities or jobs and thus income;
- *time-based exclusion* – refers to situations where other demands on time such as caring restrict the time available for travel;
- *fear-based exclusion* – where worry, fear and even terror influence how public spaces and public transport are used, particularly by women, children and the elderly; and

- *space exclusion* – where security and space management strategies can discourage socially excluded individuals from using public transport spaces.

Of course, it can be argued that transport exclusion mechanisms can be peripheral to non-transport mechanisms, but what is important to recognise is that transport, or rather the lack of access to it, can compound these factors. There is a clear need for the identification of a selection of indicators that reflect the processes linked to social exclusion and in particular, the role of transport in that exclusionary process. Indeed the idea introducing dimensions to the debate on the links between transport and social exclusion highlights the need for approaches that can identify this range of experience.

Transport Indicators and Social Exclusion

In practice transport policy makers have been slow to recognise the nature and process of social exclusion, which is reflected in the lack of suitable indicators with which to address the links between social exclusion and transport. This is clearly associated with problems connected with defining and measuring these phenomena more generally. Also, if the relationship between the different dimensions of exclusion is unclear, then it is equally as difficult to measure spatially. The problem here is that the unit of spatial measurement used will influence the geographical distribution that is observed (Church, 2000). In 2000 the then DETR sought to address these problems through an index of deprivation at local authority and ward level for England and Wales (DETR, 2000). Although this was a step forward, in that it recognised transport as a component within this, the methodology used for constructing the indices is flawed. The accessibility data incorporated in these indices is not related to either public transport service levels or to car or vehicle ownership data: it is a straight 'as the crow flies' measure of geographical distance from some very basic services such as primary school and general practitioners surgeries (Grieco, Turner and Hine, 2000). Developments in GIS and transport models represent a step forward in this area where origin and destination, mode choice and the main aspects of journey time can be mapped in low income neighbourhoods (Church et al., 2000). More generally it can be argued that a variety of indicators have been developed but there has been little attempt to relate these to access to transport systems. In 2001 the Social Exclusion Unit in announcing a renewed government interest in this area stressed the need to quantify the nature of the relationship between social exclusion and transport. For example, the Evaluation Framework Action Team of the Scottish Social Inclusion Network (established under the Social Inclusion Strategy) identified 48 indicators of social exclusion but only one of these – proportion of households without a car – was related to transport. It is this indicator that is also widely used as an indicator or proxy measure of poverty (Duguid, 1995; Gibb et al., 1998).

Typically, social exclusion is treated as a general policy aim at local government level. For example, in all three local authority areas examined in work for the Scottish Executive (Hine and Mitchell, 2001a) none of the transport authorities had indicators relating specifically to the different dimensions of exclusion for their areas. This reflects a lack of control over public transport operators with regard to the price and quantity of public transport available in areas. However, policies were in place for concessionary travel and the buying in of socially necessary public transport services. For the buying in of services it is not clear on what basis decisions are made for supporting services in this way and as a consequence it also not clear what their impact is in terms of ameliorating social exclusion. Typically, local authorities and PTEs will be more used to indicators that state the proportion of households and major facilities that are within a given distance from a bus stop (Mersey Travel, 1998). However, a succession of guidance on Local Transport Plans in England and Wales, and Local Transport Strategies in Scotland, has meant a growing awareness amongst local and transport authorities of social inclusion measures and related factors (Sinclair et al., 2001).

Emerging Themes

This book presents a number of emerging themes that are central to the debates surrounding transport disadvantage and social inclusion. These themes are discussed in more detail through out this volume, with reference to work conducted in three case study areas in the central belt of Scotland. These case studies were located in Leith (Edinburgh), Castlemilk (Glasgow) and Coatbridge (North Lanarkshire). The three areas were selected on the basis of their transport links and their socioeconomic characteristics. The work in each area involved a household survey which provided quantitative data on context-specific relationships, the experiences of different groups (in a local area context), and explores the nature of transport disadvantage in the different areas. This is supplemented by interview data gathered from the transport operators and local authorities in each of these areas.

The emerging themes discussed in this volume, which are outlined below, are important and central to how transport policy should be delivered for communities that suffer from inadequate transport links.

Public Service Failure

Poor transport services can compound the problems of living on a low income, particularly in communities that are in peripheral locations. Current approaches to dealing with public transport provision in a privatised framework amount to public service failure where operators, to maintain investment levels and profits, move away from segments of the route network to protect business on their primary routes. It is often these areas – not close to a primary route or corridor – that are left with little or no public transport provision. This can result in longer journeys on foot to get to bus stops and an increase in scheduling activity within households which may already be time-pressured and work poor in that access to child care and education may involve more planning activity at the pre-trip stage. The consequences can be that people in these circumstances find it harder to reach jobs and education facilities located in other areas of the city or its environs. Work poor and low income households may then have to do as much trip planning as a work rich household that is traditionally regarded as time poor. Local authorities fail to intervene, as they often do not have the information to help them make decisions in these circumstances or the resources to buy into those missing segments of the route network. These local authorities are also planning authorities who – often despite national guidance on the location of development at locations that can be well served by public transport – allow development on economic development grounds to occur at out of town locations which can only be satisfactorily reached by car. It is the work poor and low income households who clearly find it more difficult to access these types of opportunity.

The Uneven Impact of Transport Disadvantage

Transport disadvantage impacts to a greater extent on particular groups. The elderly, people with health problems, women, the unemployed and those on low incomes experience higher levels of transport disadvantage. Across the various dimensions of social exclusion discussed earlier in this chapter (as identified by Church et al. 1999, 2000), these groups feature disproportionately as disadvantaged when compared to the travel experiences of men, those on higher incomes and those with regular car access. This means that the future successful development of transport systems must pay attention to the needs of these groups.

Local Support Networks and the Potential of ICT

The poorest areas often receive the poorest services: public transport provision is no exception to this. In circumstances where poverty and barriers to work, such as a lack of skills, transport and child care compound the development of new services, local support networks are vital. In the three areas studied in Scotland individuals in these local communities had well developed local networks (family and friends) to whom they could turn at times of crisis and to share transport. New technology and Internet communication technology (ICT) offers ways in which support networks can be enhanced and also, for service providers, will enable services and information to be provided at a lower cost. For communities, access to ICT provides an important avenue by which service failure can be charted and participation in consultation exercises with service providers facilitated. The use of scheduling technology also allows households and service providers to match up demand and supply for goods and services in ways that may be more viable and responsive to demand.

Policy Delivery for Scatters and Clusters

This book charts the policy response in three areas in urban Scotland by local authorities to transport disadvantage in relatively deprived locations. It demonstrates clearly that local authorities lack the insights and tools to tackle these problems. In terms of developing policy responses to dealing with transport disadvantage the problem is further complicated by the nature of problem and whether it is characterised as a 'scatter' or a 'cluster'. This problem was discussed in some detail in this chapter, but essentially it places a requirement on policy makers and service providers to develop innovations that can provide solutions to the cluster or scatter problem.

Structure of the Book

The rest of this book is structured around five chapters. In Chapter 2 patterns and policies are examined. The chapter identifies the emergent themes in a highly fragmented literature and seeks to identify prevalent policies and practices.

Chapter 3 presents an introduction to the discussion of transport disadvantage in urban Scotland. For each of the case study areas used in this work this chapter provides a discussion of the policy framework, problems and nature of the areas used in the study.

Chapter 4 uses data from a household survey conducted in these case study areas to demonstrate linkages between transport access, gender and income. In Chapter 5 this link between transport disadvantage is explored further in terms of access to local services and the role of time.

In Chapter 6 the link between exclusion, the public transport network and the development of transport solutions is examined in further detail for each of the three neighbourhoods. This chapter presents material from interviews with local authorities and public transport operators in the three case study areas. Attitudes towards the public transport network, exclusion and the development transport solutions are reported on. The development of transport solutions within each case study area is also presented

Chapter 7 examines the need for new policy approaches and presents recommendations for future practice.

Chapter 2

Patterns and Practices

Introduction

Transport disadvantage and the links that can be made with social exclusion constitute an increasingly important policy area. We have seen in Chapter 1 that the very nature of transport disadvantage and social exclusion raises questions not only of the ways in which transport policy can be delivered, but also of the types of intervention that can be used to ameliorate the effect of social exclusion. The paradox here is that although this has been seen to be an important policy area, the major policy interventions have been shaped around the desire to encourage a modal shift from the private car to public transport, cycling and walking. Although improvements to public transport services can benefit non-car users and the socially excluded, there are issues about how services can best be structured to alleviate exclusion and encourage participation from those groups that have historically felt the consequences of transport disadvantage.

This chapter is concerned with patterns, practices and policies. The first part of the chapter deals with *patterns and consequences of transport related social exclusion*. This discussion focuses on the transport trends and experiences amongst those groups that are more likely to experience transport disadvantage. These are people on low incomes and the unemployed, women, the elderly and disabled, and children. This builds on a review that was undertaken for the Scottish Executive (Gaffron, Hine and Mitchell, 2001) and seeks to place the contribution of transport to social exclusion in a wider context.

The second part of this chapter – *policies and practice* – reviews policy approaches and practices that have been developed to improve the accessibility of public transport services for the excluded and transport disadvantaged.

Patterns of Transport Disadvantage

Those most likely to experience transport disadvantage are those on low incomes, women, elderly and disabled people and children (Hine and Mitchell, 2001a; DETR, 2000a). Essentially, these groups are those with traditionally lower levels of access to cars and this is at a period in time when the car is not only the dominant mode for all journeys over one mile but also plays a significant role in journeys under one mile (DETR, 1998b; RCEP, 1994). This is despite evidence from the NTS for the UK that suggests that availability of bus services has changed little over the period 1985/86 to 1995/97. In 1995/97 87 per cent of households lived within six minutes of a bus stop, compared to 86 per cent in 1985/86 (DETR, 1998b). This section examines how people from these groups travel, with the aim of informing the discussion of transport policy later in this chapter and in Chapter 6, where the policies that are needed to tackle social exclusion are discussed.

Low Income Groups

In the UK people from households on low incomes make fewer journeys overall but about twice as many journeys on foot, and three times as many journeys by bus, as those households in the two highest income deciles (Grayling, 2001). Higher income groups make more journeys by car and tend to travel further. In an analysis of data from the National Travel Survey for the periods of 1985/86 and 1996/98 it has been found that walking and bus use have declined amongst those on low incomes and that this is associated with a significant increase in car ownership (ibid.).

Although in general terms car availability increases as settlement size decreases, the greatest change in car ownership has been in the built up areas of the former metropolitan counties, where the proportion without a car fell from 53 per cent to 42 per cent over the period 1985/86 to 1995/97 (DETR, 1998b). Half of the households in the top 20 per cent income group now have two or more cars (Table 2.1). For the lowest 20 per cent income group, nearly two households in three did not have a car in 1995/97; nonetheless, this group has seen a reduction of 11 per cent in proportion of households with no car over the period 1985/6 to 1995/97.

People living in households without cars used public transport for 25 per cent of their journeys and compared to households with cars this difference in use was as much as seven times greater for those households without cars. Taxi and minicab usage are also higher amongst non-car owning households. Public transport tends to be used less by those in higher income groups (DETR, 1998b). Donald and Pickup (1991) looked at the effect of deregulation on low income families in Merseyside and concluded that fare increases were the major contributor to reduced bus use in the area (see Table 2.2).

Table 2.1 Household car ownership by income band, 1985/86 and 1995/97

Income band	1985/86			1995/97		
	No car	One car	Two or more	No car	One car	Two or more
Lowest real income	74	24	2	63	29	7
Second level	58	37	5	50	44	7
Third level	29	57	14	22	54	24
Fourth level	19	55	26	12	53	35
Highest real income	10	51	40	6	44	50

Source:Focus on Personal Travel, DETR, 1998b.

Table 2.2 Journeys per person per year by household car ownership

	Local bus	All rail	Taxi/minicab	Other public transport	All public transport	Public transport as % of all modes
Journeys per person per year						
No car	156	22	24	4	205	25
1 car	43	17	7	3	70	6
2+ cars	22	13	6	2	43	4
All households	62	17	10	3	92	9
Distance travelled per person per year						
No car	544	335	67	124	1070	43
One car	193	336	34	155	719	11
Two or more cars	124	366	39	218	746	8
All households	252	345	43	168	809	12

Source: Focus on Personal Travel, DETR, 1998b, Table 6.5

Walking remains the dominant mode of transport for people from households on low incomes, but in particular for non-car owning households, which make up to 60 per cent of households in the lowest income quintile. About 60 per cent of all journeys made by people in this group are made by people on foot (Grayling, 2001).

Women

Women have been identified as a group that experiences exclusion in a number of ways as a result of poor public transport services (Grieco, Pickup and Whipp, 1989). Hamilton et al. (2000) point out that there are clear issues affecting women's transport which relate to patterns of travel, patterns of employment, income, caring responsibilities and access to forms of travel (particularly access to cars). There are also differences amongst women in terms of the experiences of specific groups (e.g. older women, disabled women, women from ethnic minorities, women living in rural areas and lone parents). There is evidence from many parts of the world that the patterns differ including, for example, the United States (Rosenbloom, 1996), Sweden (Polk, 1996), Australia (Hanlon, 1996) and most of Africa (Grieco and Turner, 1997). Hamilton and Jenkins (1992) cite a range of reasons why women should be considered more fully by transport planners for example: multiple roles and primary responsibility for child care and domestic work, more constrained opportunities for paid employment and a much greater likelihood of being engaged in part-time and/or casual employment, usually local. Finch (Balcombe and Finch, 1984) has noted that for many women the small local area is of more significance to them as they live most of their lives bounded by the local shops, school and bus stop. As with older people and the disabled, the design of the infrastructure can mitigate against the use of a local transport system. Women with young children are perhaps hardest hit in this respect. Personal safety when using or trying to access transport infrastructure is also a major consideration for this group (DETR, 1999c; Hamilton et al., 1992).

In the UK, although evidence suggests that there is little difference between the average number of trips made by men and women, men travel much further (Hamilton and Jenkins, 1992; DETR, 1998b). In 1995/97 men made about 4 per cent more journeys per person per year than women, travelling 45 per cent further on average. Although the car is the main mode of travel for both men and women, its use is higher for men across all adult age groups. Women are also more reliant on walking and public transport than are their male counterparts. Overall 30 per cent of trips made on foot were by women, compared to 25 per cent for men. Public transport shows a similar age and sex pattern to walking. Overall, men made about 7 per cent of trips by public transport compared to 10 per cent for women. Public transport use was greatest for those aged 17–20 and over 70. One in five trips by women on public transport are made by the aged 70 and over age group (DETR, 1998b). Evidence from the Scottish Household Survey indicated that there are also differences in the frequency of driving journeys undertaken by men and women (holding driving licences), with as many as 71 per cent of men driving every day, compared to 64 per cent of women. It also showed that 77 per cent of men compared to 53 per cent of women aged over 17 held a full driving licence. There are differences at all age ranges, but this is most marked in the over 65 group, where as many as 57 per cent of women do not have access to a car, compared to 35 per cent of men. Work undertaken by System 3 (1998) showed that women took substantially more trips on foot and by public bus than men.

Commuting and business trips account for greater differences between women and men in terms of numbers of trips taken annually. Women also make more trips escorting family members to and from education. Men are more likely to travel to visit pubs and clubs, as well as sporting events. Women make more shopping trips, while the number of trips for 'personal' business is more or less identical between women and men. Women travel more during off-peak times and less after dark (Hamilton et al., 2000; DETR, 1998b).

There is mixed evidence on whether women and men exhibit differences in the complexity of the trips that they make. In the US and a number of other countries (including studies in France and the Netherlands), there appears to be clear evidence that women's travel patterns are more complex than those of men (Rosenbloom, 1989). Rosenbloom showed that women often tend to make interconnected decisions about where they work and the need to escort children to education. Women are far more likely to work closer to home, and to walk to work, but, as will become clear, this may also be linked to the lack of availability of adequate transport to enable them to take advantage of opportunities outwith the immediate local area (Reid-Howie Associates, 2000).

Up to the age of 40 younger women and men display quite similar travel patterns in terms of the actual numbers of trips taken. Beyond 40, the patterns change markedly, with women making far fewer trips overall. At a UK level, women aged 30–39 make nearly 2.2 times as many journeys of all kinds as women aged over 70, while for men of comparable ages, the figure is 1.5 times. This relates partly to the loss of the driver in the household for women who are married and became widowed, but increasingly as women restrict their travel as they become older and travel during daylight hours, using known routes (Hamilton et al., 2000; Reid-Howie Associates, 2000). Younger women are also more likely to have a full driving licence (Scottish Executive, 2001; DETR, 1998). Proportionately, older women make far more journeys on foot and by bus or coach, and, inevitably (given their lower levels of labour market participation), older women make a much higher percentage of their trips for shopping and other leisure purposes (Reid-Howie Associates, 2000). There are also differences based on income. Among women in 'high income areas', 80 per cent have a licence, whereas among women in council-rented flats, the comparable level is only 21 per cent. Lone parents do, however, make more trips overall, and where there are male/female households there is no evidence of change to the pattern whereby the male partner is the main driver (Hamilton et al., 2000; Scottish Executive, 2001).

Some studies have identified different travel patterns among women from ethnic minorities (GLC, 1984). Hamilton, Jenkins and Gregory (1991) showed that women from ethnic minorities in West Yorkshire tended to travel further on average than other groups of women, in order to travel to specialist shops, see family members and attend places of worship.

Other studies relating to the gender specific restrictions on time budgets experienced by women have already been discussed. Obviously such restrictions would apply equally to men carrying out the same tasks, i.e. child care combined with general household chores. These tasks often require complicated trip chaining (Turner et al., 1998), which may in some cases be impossible due to the lack of suitable means of transport or the discrepancies between personal and transport schedules. Gaerling et al. (1998) pointed out that the associated time pressures and stress caused by multiple and potentially conflicting demands (particularly salient for those without recourse to the use of a car) can bring with them additional adverse health effects, thus exacerbating the effect of exclusion, which limitations in mobility are already imposing.

Older People

In the developed world it has come to be appreciated that people are living longer and the population of elderly people is living longer (Olshansky et al., 1993; Cohen, 1996; ONS, 1998). In Scotland the share of older people in the population is set to rise considerably (GROS, 1997).

Older people use the car less than other age groups and as result bus use is higher. Walking accounts for a large proportion of trips, particularly for those in the 60–70 age group, but after the age of 70 this declines as the reduced ability to walk becomes a more important factor. Car ownership is lower among older people and this is partly due to lower incomes amongst the retired (Lavery et al., 1992; Bly, 1993). Analysis of NTS data over the period 1975 to 1991 indicates that the percentage of older people will increase in terms of licence-holding as present licence-holders move into older age groups (Bly, 1993). Partly as a result of these trends, older people feature disproportionately in road casualty data. In 1992 for people aged over 75, 58 per cent of killed or seriously injured were pedestrians. The likelihood of a pedestrian accident is three times as high for people aged over 70 as for people aged between 30 and 50.

Hopkin et al. (1978) found walking amongst elderly people to be the most frequent means of travel. Car ownership increased the number of journeys per day to 1.27 for drivers and 0.94 for non-drivers in households with a car compared with 0.76 for people in households without a car. Rosenbloom (1992) similarly found that trip rates were higher for older people aged 71 to 75 and for those aged 85 compared to those without drivers' licences. Other studies have identified the difficulties that older people have in walking, including uneven pavements, hills, ramps, traffic and crossing roads, steps and carrying bags (Hopkin et al., 1978; Hillman and Whalley, 1979; Hitchcock and Mitchell, 1984; Leake et al., 1991; National Consumer Council, 1987).

Disabled People

Disabled people are a group that also features in discussions surrounding the link between transport and social exclusion (Hine and Mitchell, 2001; DETR, 2000). They suffer because, for a variety of reasons, they find it difficult to access public services. These reasons include low income, physical layout of infrastructure and design of vehicles, and location of stops. The restructuring of bus services to the edges of residential and commercial areas on main transport corridors could potentially have a profound effect on this group. There is, however, little evidence to suggest the extent and nature of such service restructuring exercises on this group.

Estimates suggest that about 10 per cent of the population of Europe suffer from some form of impairment (ECMT, 1986), more recent surveys have however increased this estimate to between 12–14 per cent (Mitchell, 1997). Data for Britain suggest that the proportion of the population who are disabled now is 14.2 per cent (Martin et al. 1988, 1989). Work has been undertaken that has identified the capabilities of the population, the numbers using different types of mobility aid and the proportions of people capable of performing a wide variety of tasks including walking certain distances, climbing steps and balancing (Harris, 1971; Martin et al., 1988). This work has also been extended to look at these capabilities in relation to bus use (Brooks et al., 1974; Flores et al., 1981; Oxley and Benwell, 1985; Mitchell, 1988).

Numerous surveys have highlighted the problems of mobility-impaired people. Borjesson (1989) in a survey of travel in Sweden found that disabled people travel less frequently, while in Canada and the US it has been estimated that about 5 per cent of the population aged over 65 and older were transport handicapped (Systems Approach Consultants Ltd, 1979; US Department of Transportation, 1978). Abt Associates (1969) found that in the Boston area handicapped people made 1.13 intra-regional trips per day compared with 2.23 trips per day for the general population. Fewer handicapped people were licensed to drive, fewer were employed and more were poor, with an income of less than $4,000 p.a.

Work has also demonstrated that the distances some disabled people are able to travel are very limited. GLAD (1986) in a survey of transport handicapped people in London found that 34 per cent of them could not walk more than one-quarter of a mile alone without experiencing discomfort. Oxley and Alexander (1994) found that 30 per cent of disabled residents in London could walk less than 50 yards. Leake et al. (1991) found that found that between 50–80 per cent of disabled people (including wheelchair users, visually impaired, stick users and ambulatory unaided) could not move with assistance more than 180m without a rest. More recently, work on visually impaired people has found that they have higher frequencies of accidents than sighted people (Gallon et al., 1995).

Studies have also identified the problems experienced by the disabled and mobility impaired in relation to their use of bus services. This includes waiting, boarding and moving around the bus (GLAD, 1986; Fowkes et al. 1987; Oxley and Benwell, 1985; Oxley and Alexander, 1994; Mitchell, 1988). This work has resulted in the adoption of standards for vehicles.

Children

Children are a group that do need to be considered in discussions of transport and social exclusion. Data from the recent Scottish study on transport and social exclusion and the DETR study in England have however largely ignored the problems that children encounter on their journeys and the consequences of this in terms of access to goods and services and participation in key activities. What we do know is that child pedestrians are profoundly disadvantaged in a transport system designed for adults. Save the Children Scotland recently released the findings of a study on children's views on transport, which included a section on transport and social exclusion. This section explored the extent to which transport plays a role in hindering or enhancing the ability of young people to participate in society and take up opportunities. The study found that 'secondary school pupils and young trainees expressed awareness of employment, educational and personal horizons being reduced by costly and inaccessible transport services' (Tyrell, 2000).

Pedestrian accident data have shown that children in the poorest areas and lower economic and social groups are more likely to be killed and seriously injured than children in higher socioeconomic groups (Abdalla et al., 1997). A study in Birmingham also found that Asian children aged less than 9 years old were twice as likely to be injured as pedestrians as their non-Asian counterparts (Lawson and Edwards, 1991). This difference was attributed to the housing location and situation of these Asian families, i.e. inner city areas with low levels of provision for play space. Preston (1972), in an analysis of child pedestrian accidents in Manchester and Salford, found strong connections between the injury rate, index of overcrowding and an index of social class, noting that (p. 329) 'the overcrowded house is likely to be in an overcrowded street, without gardens or play spaces for children'. Yet this needs to be treated with caution (as Preston also noted at the time) because the areas that exhibited overcrowding were not randomly distributed throughout the catchments area sampled, but tended to cluster around the city centre. These areas are more likely to experience high levels of traffic and this traffic density is likely to be a product of population density. Other studies have suggested that maternal preoccupation could be a factor that contributes to higher levels of child pedestrian casualties (Backett and Johnson, 1959; Read et al., 1963).

Hillman et al. (1990) in a study of children's independent mobility found that independent travel by schoolchildren had declined markedly over the period 1971–90. This was found to be a result of parent's fears for the safety of their children. This has resulted in a significant increase in the number of children who are escorted to all destinations, especially by car (Tranter, 1996). The reduction in independent mobility may have significant impacts on their intellectual and psychological development (van Vliet, 1983; Kegerris, 1993; Elliot, 1985). Others have commented that independent mobility is important, as walking and cycling journeys to school or other destinations provide genuine play activities and an opportunity to discover their physical environment (Engwicht, 1992; De Monchaux, 1981).

Consequences of Transport Disadvantage

Barriers to Employment

Lack of transport is an important barrier to employment opportunities (Hine and Mitchell, 2001; Audit Commission, 1999; Rural Development Commission, 1999). Cost and availability of childcare, lack of knowledge of the local job market and an unwillingness to travel outside the locality can also be barriers to employment (Burkett, 2000; DfEE, 1999). Many studies have also been undertaken that examine the variety of barriers to employment including job search behaviour and the structure of local economies (Gorter et al., 1993; Lawless, 1995). Other work has looked at the spatial mismatch hypothesis in terms of residential location, transport costs and work in suburbia (Arnott, 1998). Work in the US has also indicated that spatial isolation is strongly associated with higher unemployment rates amongst black youth (O'Regan and Quigley, 1998). Holzer et al. (1994) found that high travel costs and reduced travel distances appear to raise unemployment durations and lower wages for blacks by modest amounts. The study also found that blacks and inner city residents do not offset greater metropolitan decentralisation with greater distances being travelled. Further evidence from the US for the Washington metropolitan region suggests that, for those in employment, jobs and housing mutually co-locate to optimise travel times (Levinson and Kumar, 1994). An examination of the geography of unemployment and economic inactivity in Britain raised concerns about the increasing isolation of those unemployed resulting from the contraction of the manufacturing sector (Green, 1995). Zhang and Dickson (2000) have commented that a mismatch between areas where new jobs have been created and the location of existing public transport networks contributes to an exclusion from job opportunities for those who rely on public transport.

A study in Alberta, Edmonton found that in the case of the urban poor, women have shorter work trips and a greater preference for part-time jobs than men because of their childcare and household responsibilities (Mensah, 1995). Dasgupta (1982a, 1982b, 1983) found that employment opportunities in the inner and outer areas of Manchester were influenced by the choice of transport used. Other studies have identified similar links. Green (1998) found that in the London Boroughs of Hackney and Islington the lack of transport and of local jobs were the main factors contributing to poor access to employment. McGregor and McConnachie (1995) cite the same two factors as contributing to the concentration of unemployment in disadvantaged housing areas.

Recently work has also suggested that on the disadvantaged housing estates the economic reality is sharply defined by the resource constraints of childcare, travel to work time, cost and availability. Particularly when confronted by low wages and an increasing proportion of part-time work, travel to work costs may make taking a low income job an uneconomic option (McGregor et al., 1998). Similarly, a House of Commons Select Committee on Education and Employment found that lack of access to travel created a barrier for lone parents getting to work. As a consequence they recommended the introduction of travel subsidies (Select Committee on Education and Employment, 1998).

A number of studies have also focused on the links between access to transport and employment in rural areas. Studies of young people growing up in rural parts of North Yorkshire have found that most of the young people needed their own transport to hold down work, while public transport was seen to be unreliable and timetables did not match up with work schedules (Monk et al., 1999; Stafford et al., 1999; Moseley, 1979). Other work in rural Scotland found that limited public transport was a major issue for young people in both areas. It was commonly found that young families had one car that the husband took to work. This often left women and young children isolated and without transport throughout the day (Pavis et al., 2000).

Exclusion from Services

Recent work for the UK government by the Social Exclusion Unit found that transport and individual mobility was mentioned to some degree by many of their policy action teams as a reason why problems were experienced by poorer communities (Social Exclusion Unit, 2001). Lack of readily-available transport, whether car or public transport, has a clear impact on whether particular goods and services can be accessed. In the case of public transport, the problem – especially for communities with low levels of car ownership – is that services are more likely to be located on transport corridors. When combined with timetables that do not accommodate new forms of employment (e.g. shiftwork), this means that access can be problematic and that temporal barriers to job markets have been created (Hine and Scott, 2001).

Work by Leyshon and Thrift (1995) has highlighted the difficulties experienced by those living in disadvantaged areas in terms of their ability to access financial services. A recent review by the Centre for Research into Socially Inclusive Services (Sinclair, 2001) found that there was a need to understand more fully issues associated with financial inclusion and access to local goods and services. Young (1999) has highlighted the difficulties in accessing healthcare facilities for women in low income groups due to low levels of car ownership and reliance on public transport. Lack of transport and the cost of public transport have been cited as significant barriers to further education (DfEE, 1998; Callender, 1999).

Fear and Perceptions of Safety

Perceptions of safety and fear can have significant effects on levels of personal mobility. Older people, women and those from ethnic communities are more likely to fear crime while using public transport (Crime Concern and Transport and Travel Research, 1997). Other work has found that people feel markedly safer when walking around their neighbourhood during the day compared to after dark. Women feel less safe than men and are more worried about being a victim of street crime (Crime Concern, 1999a). Studies by Atkins (1989) and Pain (1997) have highlighted the problems experienced by women when travelling. Behaviours were found include avoidance of making a trip, especially in the dark. Work has also identified a fear of interchange facilities and stations in the dark and at off-peak periods, and the need for a security presence in these locations (Hine and Scott, 2001).

The consequence of this fear is that trips are either not made or that alternative arrangements are made where it is possible to avoid these situations. In their work on perceptions of the public transport journey in Scotland, Hine and Scott (2001) found that switches from bus to car were often a result of these fears and the inability of the services to meet shift patterns. Other work has found that taxis can play a very important role in these circumstances (Pain, 1997; Hine and Mitchell, 2001b). For younger people, studies have found that the anxieties experienced when using public transport are similar to those of adults. Young women feel very unsafe after dark when using public transport (Crime Concern, 1999b).

Policies and Practices

Traditionally policy interventions into this area have emerged from the specialist transport provider who has sought to address those gaps in provision not filled by mainstream transport providers. Other interventions have resulted from the need to introduce concessionary travel for older and disabled people and the growth of guidance and legislation on these matters. These responses have, however, largely been in the public domain and recommendations for reducing barriers experienced by the socially excluded rarely come from the private sector. For example, the coordination of private transport through car clubs as a mechanism for overcoming social exclusion has not been addressed. The following sections highlight aspects of those interventions that are a feature of the policy environment in this area. Taken together, these studies suggest that transport disadvantage can contribute to the process of exclusion for individuals and communities by either further worsening conditions experienced or by starting the process of exclusion (Gaffron et al., 2001; Hine and Mitchell, 2001; Lucas et al., 2001).

Specialist Services

Specialist services are typically provided by the voluntary sector. These services typically consist of: group hire bus services; dial-a-ride services and voluntary car schemes (DETR, 1999b).

The objectives of dial-a-ride services were originally to provide a demand responsive service serving low-density suburban areas. As a concept they have been around in the UK since the early 1970s. Initial experiments with this form of transport found that the services were expensive and failed to cater for dispersed trip patterns (Oxley, 1977; DETR, 1999b). Despite this, the approach remains an accepted method of delivering services to the elderly and disabled; a section of the population where transport needs can be expensive (Mitchell, 1997; Byrne and Holt, 1995; Speller and Mitchell, 1975; SAMPLUS, 1999). The efficiency of dial-a-ride systems has been improved by computerised scheduling packages that in effect provide the operator of services with a reservation system for services. Beuret (1994) has suggested that taxis offer immediacy and flexibility, criteria that are lacking in dial-a-ride services.

Ling and Mannion (1995), in an evaluation of dial-a-ride in the northeast of England, revealed that schemes can improve the quality of life positively for older people across six dimensions: independence, loneliness, morale and life satisfaction, health and absence of pain, financial welfare and activity participation. Gaffron et al. (2001) found little or no work which has explored the specific contribution of needs-based transport initiatives to weakening exclusion mechanisms and assessing their impact on time/space organisation of individuals, households and facilities. Analysis of the effects of these schemes tends to be in terms of attractiveness to passengers and operational monitoring of such schemes (Tyson, 1995; Harman and Thatcher, 1995).

Another specialist transport concept is the 'service route'. This is concerned with bringing the bus service closer to the residents (Stahl, 1992) and as such represents a move away from traditional route planning, which is based on radial routes coming into a city or town centre. The service route is a regular route network but the route is based on where the proportions of elderly and disabled people live and important destinations such as health centres, hospitals and shops (Stahl, 1992; Evans and Smyth, 1997). These schemes have been implemented internationally in Denmark, Finland, Norway and Holland, Canada and the US. Stahl (1992) and, in a later paper, Stahl and Brundell-Freij (1995) provide some evaluations of these routes. The evidence indicates that they are cost-effective and reduce the need for specialist transport.

Taxis

Taxis are the most flexible transport service (Beuret, 1994, 1995; McLary, 1995) and are a popular alternative to other modes of transport. The DETR has noted that taxis are the most expensive form of transport in the UK, on average five to seven times more expensive than other modes per passenger mile. To combat the high cost, taxi card schemes exist as a subsidy for travel by this mode (Trench and Lister, 1994). Two forms of taxi operation have developed. Essentially these are taxis run through voluntary driver schemes and those operated by commercial firms. Voluntary car schemes have been concerned with transporting people for social services, health and education purposes, however this role has expanded to shopping and leisure-based trips (DETR, 1999b). These schemes have been effective although funding and volunteer resources do dictate their availability, which is restricted according to specific eligibility criteria (DETR, 1999b). Beuret (1995) outlined a number of shortcomings with taxis, including problems accessing vehicles for those with disabilities and wheelchairs, although a number of companies are pioneering wheelchair-accessible vehicles. Beuret also noted that those groups in the population that tend to use taxis the most also tend to be on lower incomes, although there has been a growth in their usage by the general population for leisure purposes. A number of authors have commented on other features of the taxi systems where improvements can be made to facilitate easier use, including accessible taxi ranks located near key facilities, use of black cab design vehicles rather than conventional vehicles, and smart card technology, not only for ease of use but also so that a record of concessions used can be kept (DETR, 1999; Beuret, 1995).

Bus Policies

Low income households spend more on bus fares than on rail fares (Grayling, 2001). In comparison, rail fares are more expensive for those on low incomes. An established method of improving access to bus services is through a general or targeted subsidy. The 1985 Transport Act, which deregulated bus services in Great Britain, heralded the end of low fares policies: in other words, passenger transport authorities and local authorities could no longer subsidise bus services except those that were deemed to be socially necessary and unprofitable. Donald and Pickup (1991) found that deregulation in Merseyside and resultant fare increases were the main cause of reduced use. More recently, there has been some movement on this under the Transport Act 2000 (2001 in Scotland) where quality contracts allow local transport authorities to set fares within a franchise. Such interventions that produce a general fare subsidy would be a positive step for low income groups.

Until recently there has been limited evidence to suggest the benefits of this approach for low income groups. Work has suggested that the cost of subsidies and fare reduction are less than has been previously thought (Grayling, 2001). A fare reduction in metropolitan areas in money and time savings to passengers and other road users could outweigh the costs of the subsidy. This approach is, however, not possible, due to the deregulated system, but could be implemented through quality contracts (Hine and Mitchell, 2001; Grayling, 2001).

Targeted subsidies offer another approach that is used to grant concessionary travel to pensioners, the disabled, children under 16 and students aged up to 18 years in full-time education. Research indicates that these schemes encourage travel – those with concessions travel more often and further (O'Reilly, 1989, 1990; Bonsall and Dunkerley, 1997). Nonetheless, it is possible for other groups to be included in a concessionary scheme on a voluntary basis (Grayling, 2001).

Improving the accessibility of services is another aspect of bus policy. The Disability Discrimination Act 1995, which legislates for mainstream public transport to become accessible to the disabled and wheelchair users, when combined with local transport strategies and quality partnerships will ensure a fleet of accessible vehicles. The adaptation of street infrastructure, including bus boarders and raised platforms, upgrading of bus shelters, and the enforcement of parking restrictions in bus lanes and around bus stops, is also an important component of this approach (York and Balcombe, 1997; Evans and Smyth, 1997).

Conclusion

Transport disadvantage can have important impacts on daily life, for example in terms of access to goods and services. Those most likely to experience this disadvantage and the process of social exclusion are those on low incomes, women, the elderly, disabled people and children. This chapter has highlighted these patterns of disadvantage. Importantly, evidence indicates that policy makers and research studies have tended to ignore children in this work.

The consequences of transport-related social exclusion can be widely felt. Lack of transport or transport disadvantage can result in barriers to employment opportunities and spatial isolation. Work has also highlighted how the lack of access to a private car, when combined with the closure of local services, e.g. banks and post offices, can heighten this feeling of exclusion. Public transport can be avoided for personal security reasons; however, those with no other choices can be disadvantaged in terms of how often they are able to access facilities.

The chapter presented information on policies and approaches that are typically adopted where barriers to transport are found to exist. It is clear that there is a wealth of information on specific interventions but little evidence of any evaluation of their impact on weakening transport based social exclusion. Nonetheless there is a range of interventions that can be used to target particular problems. Hine and Mitchell (2001) noted, however, that there was need for an integration of systems and approaches.

Chapter 3

Circumstance and Policy Context: Leith, Castlemilk and Coatbridge

Introduction

Undeniably, policy concerns at this time have been principally that of car dependence and modal shift – the switch from private car to public transport (DETR, 1998a; Hine and Scott, 2001). The dilemma for policy and practice is the marriage of these objectives as now enshrined in statute, as for example in the Transport Act (Scotland) 2001, and the reduction of social exclusion through improvements to transport infrastructure. This chapter establishes the circumstances and policy context of three case study areas: Leith in Edinburgh, Castlemilk in Glasgow and Coatbridge in North Lanarkshire. Information presented in this chapter also extends to a description of the population and their characteristics in terms of tenure, household structure, income, health and perception of neighbourhood.

The three case study areas discussed in this and subsequent chapters were selected for their differing urban locations – Leith as an urban district located close to a city centre with good bus links, Castlemilk as an estate located on the periphery of a city, and Coatbridge as a free-standing town that has employment opportunities on the edge of the town, such as industrial parks that are more accessible by car, but inaccessible for those relying on public transport. The 1991 travel to work census data shows Lanarkshire (formerly Monklands local authority) as having the lowest proportion using bus to travel to work and, of the three areas, the highest proportions travelling to work by car (Table 3.1). A household survey was undertaken in each of these areas to establish in more detail the nature of transport disadvantage and the characteristics of the populations living in these areas.[1]

City Centre – Leith, Edinburgh

Historically a port, Leith is situated to the north of Edinburgh city centre and is relatively well served by public transport routes. The ward selected for the

Table 3.1   Mode choice, journey to work 1991 population census

Mode	City of Edinburgh		City of Glasgow		Monklands	
	N	%	*N*	%	*N*	%
Train	178	0.9	1,291	5.8	198	5.3
Bus	5,903	31.0	6,864	30.8	541	14.5
Car driver	7,514	39.5	7,755	34.9	1,742	46.8
Car passenger	1,100	5.8	1,663	7.5	549	14.8
Bicycle	346	1.8	167	0.7	7	0.1
Walking	2,744	14.5	2,860	12.8	506	13.6
Total*	18,989		22,221		3,717	

*   Total applies to all modes and is based on 10 per cent sample of 1991 population census.
The table presented here has been abbreviated to include the most important modes for
the journey to work in these areas.

purposes of the survey was Harbour, which encompasses Warriston,
Bonnington and is a part of what might be described as central Leith. The
population in Harbour ward is 6,990. The area has three major concentrations
of shopping with significant comparison goods shopping content; two of which
(Leith Walk, and Leith Central) fall within the case study area. These are
supplemented by other groups of shops, predominantly convenience shops,
which serve a local or neighbourhood need (Figure 3.1). A number of problems
for residents in the area were found to exist, despite the view held by operators
and the local authority that the density of the public transport bus network
was high. These were principally the feeling of isolation from other areas of
the city, restricted services at the weekends which often made public transport
unsuitable in terms of accessing jobs due the nature of the shift pattern, time
taken to travel principally due to traffic congestion, cost and the physical
inaccessibility of vehicles (Hine and Mitchell, 2001).

There are no local train services within Leith itself. However, there are a
number of bus routes in this area operated mainly by Lothian Buses (formerly
Lothian Regional Transport (LRT)) and also by First Edinburgh. Within the
case study area, the majority of these services are concentrated on two main
streets: Leith Walk and Great Junction Street. More recently these two
companies have been in fierce competition for the lucrative main corridor
routes across the city.[2] Several taxi and private hire car companies also operate
in Leith. These operators participate in the taxi-card scheme which entitles
the bearer to a £3.00 discount on taxi fares. The card holder is limited to 104
single journeys per year (equivalent to one return journey a week), although

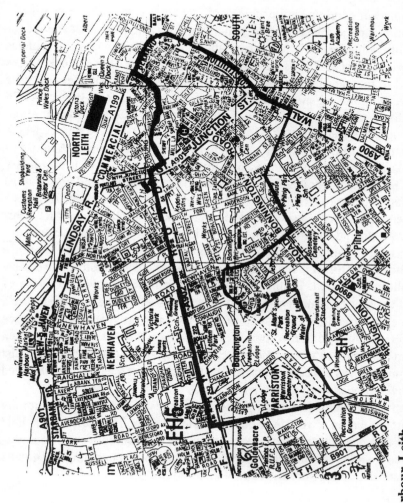

Figure 3.1 Harbour, Leith

Source: Reproduced by permission of Geographers' A–Z Map Co. Ltd. Licence No. B1737. This product includes mapping data licensed from Ordnance Survey ®. © Crown Copyright 2002. Licence number 100017302.

these can be used at any time (e.g. all within the first six months, if desired). Users must be registered disabled and unable to use public transport.

Several organisations provide community transport within the Edinburgh city area. These include those organising statutory provision for the disabled, such as Edinburgh City Council, who administer concessions to the elderly and disabled in addition to the 'taxi-card' scheme. Handicabs, a charitable organisation, operate 'Dial-a-Ride' which provides a door-to-door service for people with limited mobility who are unable to use ordinary buses. All vehicles are wheelchair accessible. This service operates seven days a week, but is restricted to those resident in Edinburgh or the Lothians. All users must be registered with the organisation, although registration is free. It costs £1.75 for the first three miles and £0.25 per mile thereafter. Journeys further afield may be more expensive. Handicabs also operate 'Dial-a-Bus', a service which provides transport from a client's home to local shopping centres. Again, this service is for people with limited mobility who are unable to use ordinary buses. The service operates in certain areas on certain days and places must be booked in advance. It costs £0.55 per mile (Hine and Mitchell, 2001).

Other community transport services include a library link bus which takes library users to and from their home to the local library. The service operates once every fortnight. The library also provides a delivery service for those users who cannot travel to the library. Both services are available to the elderly and mobility impaired. Lothian Community Transport provide the hire of vehicles to other community transport operators – vehicles are available on a self-drive basis or with a driver. This organisation also provides training advice and information to other voluntary service operators who run their own transport services, or those who are considering doing so. Some specialist care centres such as day centres and residential homes for the elderly or disabled also provide transport to their clients (ibid.).

Despite the many organisations across the city that provide community transport there is no or very little coordination of effort. The view largely held within the community transport sector is that the local authority and operators do not see the role for community transport organisations becoming any greater in terms of delivering services to excluded groups.

Policy Context

Despite there being no interventions by the local authority in the form of subsidised services for the Leith area, the City of Edinburgh Council have been proactive in promoting and developing strategies and policies within their local transport strategy that seek to tackle transport-related social exclusion. The local transport strategy states: 'Lack of access to facilities and services is a fundamental facet of social exclusion. Social exclusion results from the existence of barriers that make it difficult or impossible for people to participate fully in society' (City of Edinburgh Council, 2001, p. 101). The strategy goes on to identify those groups that are more likely to suffer from transport related social exclusion. These groups include the elderly, disabled, poorer people, women, children, parents with children, and and shoppers with heavy bags (ibid.; Hine and Mitchell, 2001). In the interim strategy the report sought to explore internal and external barriers to transport related social exclusion. Hine and Mitchell (2001) commented that internal barriers are presented as non-access to car use, difficulty coping with traffic and difficulty accessing non-car transport (including walking and cycling as well as public transport). External barriers are presented as the concentration of facilities and services, especially if the locations are hard to access by public transport, foot and cycle, cost of transport, detailed road design issues (e.g. lack of dropped kerbs), heavy and/or fast traffic, inaccessible vehicle design, infrequent public transport services and long distances from home to public transport services.

Most noticeably the council have established a Transport and Social Exclusion Task Force with representatives from the Social Work Department, Education, City Development Departments and from the voluntary, disability and mental health sectors. This task force produced a report (April 2000) with a series of recommendations on how the LTS could seek to address the transport needs of the socially excluded or essentially promote social inclusion. This work has also been augmented by the Lord Provost's Commission on Social Exclusion. This body recommended that comprehensive public transport links should be provided from all areas to major facilities and centres of employment; and that by June 2002 a Task Force should be created to review the impact of national transport policies on disabled people in Edinburgh; and, finally that the physical accessibility of public transport in Edinburgh should be investigated.

Within the Local Transport Strategy the explicit policy commitments made under the subheading of social exclusion are as follows:

1. Make a presumption that all new transport projects and infrastructure will have accessibility 'built in' from the outset. This approach will also be applied to all upgrades of existing systems, and, where applicable, to simple maintenance and renewal initiatives.

2. Maintain funding for those schemes which are specifically targeted at people with specific mobility needs, including bus and taxi concessions and Handicabs.
3. In appraising future transport investments, the council will explicitly evaluate the benefits and costs to socially excluded groups (City of Edinburgh Council, 2001, p. 103).

The Local Transport Strategy also consists of a number of programmes targeted specifically at transport-related social exclusion. These include, in the short term, investigating the role that people (staff or escorts) can play in reducing social exclusion, possibly through agencies such as WRVS, LCTS and the Social Work Department. These people would act as 'travel trainers', to help those who can use low floor buses for the first time, but who may lack the confidence to do so. Other programmes include the expansion of the availability of the dial-a-bus network and investigation of such measures as the introduction of shared taxi services and reduction of fares per passenger. In the medium-to long-term, the council will consider interest-free loans for bus season tickets for those returning to the labour market, and promoting season tickets to certain job seekers for limited periods (City of Edinburgh Council, 2001).

Peripheral Housing Estate – Castlemilk, Glasgow

Castlemilk is a large peripheral housing estate with a population of 18,000, and is located to the south of Glasgow city. The Castlemilk ward itself has a population of 8,683 (Census, 1991). This area, long characterised by deprivation, has been a priority area for public investment and regeneration for some time. The Castlemilk Partnership was set up in 1988 as part of the New Life Urban Partnerships to tackle problems associated with the high unemployment levels, lack of essential facilities available, poor housing and derelict land, the high levels of crime and low education attainment that characterised the area.

Transport links have been an issue of concern in relation to the accessibility of employment opportunities and shopping facilities in surrounding areas.[3] In Castlemilk itself there had previously been problems with access to decent shopping provision in the past and people depended on transport links to the nearest shopping area in Rutherglen. This has changed with the introduction of Kwiksave, a supermarket chain, and the increased take up of small business units within the central shopping area. In previous studies of the area, access to employment opportunities has also been highlighted as an issue for concern and, subsequently, pilot transport initiatives have been introduced to improve the links between Castlemilk and East Kilbride.

There has never been a railway in Castlemilk itself. The closest railway stations are at Croftfoot and Kingspark, from where services operate mainly to Central Station in Glasgow city centre. Both train stations are accessible by bus services running into the city centre. These stations are on the Cathcart Circle, which links Glasgow Central to different communities on the south side of Glasgow, namely Shawlands, Langside, Mount Florida, Muirend and Neilston. Services run on average every 20 to 30 minutes. There are no designated cycle routes provided in Castlemilk. There are a number of taxi and private hire cars operating in the Castlemilk area. There is a taxi rank situated in the centre of Castlemilk outside the shopping centre.

There are a number of bus services operating in the Castlemilk area which incorporate different routes throughout the case study area. These are provided in the main by FirstGlasgow, First Stop Travel and Dart Buses. The majority of these services operate seven days.[4]

On all bus services, fares can be paid direct to the driver (no change given). Reduced rates apply to juveniles between the ages of five and 16. Holders of concessionary travel cards can obtain concessionary travel at the times stated on their travel cards. There is no information provided on the fare stages or costs of a specific journey in the timetables, although the following information was found on the number of concession passes or tickets offered by FirstGlasgow which apply to the services operating in the Castlemilk area and the Coatbridge area:

- a 'First Value' ticket offers an off peak adult day return for £1.50 which is valid for travel city-wide, after 9.30am, Monday to Friday. The same ticket but for travel network-wide costs £1.90;
- the 'Transfer 90' ticket costs £1.30 and is valid for interchange within 90 minutes of boarding the first bus. The same conditions apply where the ticket can only be used off-peak, i.e. after 9.30am, Monday to Friday, and all day at weekends;
- the FirstGlasgow travel pass starts at £7.00 (dependent on zones) and allows unlimited travel, seven days per week, 24 hours per day.

Community transport provision is similar to that in Leith. Strathclyde Passenger Transport provide a dial-a-bus service to people with a mobility impairment who are unable to use public transport. The service costs £0.40 per single

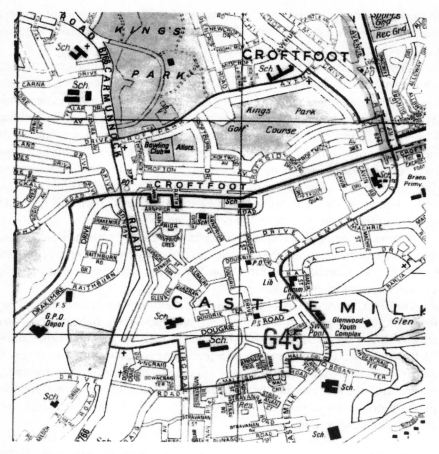

Figure 3.2   Castlemilk

Source: Reproduced by permission of Geographers' A–Z Map Co. Ltd. Licence No. B1737. This product includes mapping data licensed from Ordnance Survey ®. © Crown Copyright 2002. Licence number 100017302.

journey for concession card holders and £0.60 for non-concession card holders. There is an application procedure where an independent health assessor evaluates each case. The following restrictions however apply to the use of this service:

• journeys must be booked one day in advance. Bookings are taken from 9am to 11.45am, Monday to Friday. Bookings for Monday travel are made on a Friday;

- can only be used for journeys within Castlemilk;
- cannot be used to attend hospital appointments.

Hine and Mitchell (2001) found that one local community group (Castlemilk Community Transport) provides hire of vehicles to groups and projects within the Castlemilk area – available with drivers or for self-drive. Vehicles must be booked in advance and there is no limit on time or distance. Vehicles are available all year round except Christmas (since all their drivers are volunteers). It is possible that other local community groups, of which there are many based in Castlemilk, provide transport to their client groups.

Policy Context

The Glasgow City Council interim Local Strategy is presented as a series of documents relating to transport issues in Glasgow. The documents include the 'Keep Glasgow Moving. Draft Consultation', 'Transportation Initiatives Report' and 'Keep Glasgow Moving. Consultation Analysis'. The pack also included the Transport Strategy produced by Strathclyde Passenger Transport in 1997. The presentation is significantly different from that of the City of Edinburgh Council and reflects the division of responsibilities between the Passenger Transport Authority, responsible for public transport, and the City Council where the remit is for highways and land use planning.

Hine and Mitchell (2001) noted that, despite a considerable wealth of information included in these documents, it was nonetheless difficult to identify a specific commitment to promoting inclusion as a policy objective and the means through which this could be achieved. Although not explicitly addressed, there is a commitment to providing affordable public transport and an integrated transport system. The Council also state that an affordable public transport system has a role to play in regenerating Glasgow's economy and increasing job opportunities.

However, there is a need to be able to identify and assess the existence of barriers and their impact upon the accessibility of the transport system in order to aid a clearer understanding of their impact on accessibility of facilities and opportunities for people in society. Clearly, this impact is affected by the planning and land use policy of any given area, while lack of choice in transport can exclude people from opportunities enjoyed by the majority of society.

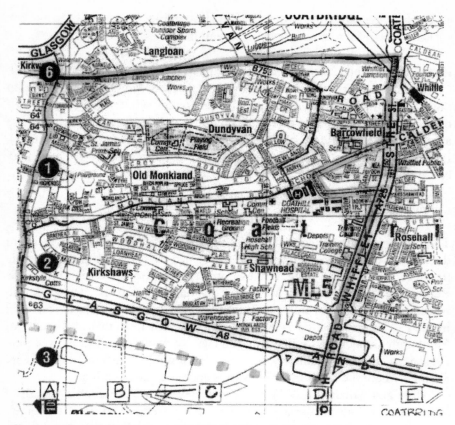

Figure 3.3   Kirkshaws and Old Monkland, Coatbridge

Free-standing town – Coatbridge, North Lanarkshire

Coatbridge is situated nine miles east of Glasgow and is a former industrial town with a population of 43,617 (Census 1991). The area is considered to be served by 'adequate' transport links during the day. However, evening and Sunday services are thought to be poor. There is also some recognition that public transport services do not necessarily meet the shift patterns of local factories.[5] The data collected for this study area indicated that restricted public transport services meant that people found it difficult to attend leisure facilities. Public transport services also did not coincide with shift patterns for some workers and many found the services costly. Access to travel information for the area was difficult and respondents found it difficult to access surrounding areas such as Cumbernauld. This case study area had the highest levels of car use and this seems to be symptomatic of poor bus services.

The wards of Kirkshaws and Old Monkland used in the household survey are situated to the south of the main town and have a population of 10,043 (Census, 1991). The boundaries of the electoral wards encompass different housing estates and an industrial estate. There are some small local grocery shops and a post office situated within the housing estates. The main shopping facilities, public library and other amenities, such as the health centre, are situated to the north of the area around the main street of Coatbridge. The area was chosen as it has particularly poor employment opportunities and poor transport links to surrounding areas, such as Livingston and edge of town industrial parks, which have opportunities for employment.

South Coatbridge has been described as one of the largest single areas of multiple deprivation in North Lanarkshire; and consequently, has recently been designated as a Social Inclusion Partnership area. South Coatbridge is an area characterised by high levels of unemployment, with less employees in full-time work, very low numbers of self-employed and low numbers of students in further education. The area has a considerably higher than average number of lone parent families, increased levels of permanently sick and significantly higher than average proportion of people with long term illness. Very low owner occupation rates and significantly low levels of car ownership are also characteristic of the area.

Coatbridge town is well served by rail links, although the nearest train stations to the case study area are Whifflet station, situated to the northeast of the area, or Kirkwood station, situated to the northwest. Neither station is particularly accessible for the residents of the area although there is a bus link to Whifflet station. The main service operating on this line to Glasgow Central with stops at Carmyle, Mount Vernon, Baillieston, Bargeddie and Kirkwood.

The bus services operating in the Kirkshaws and Old Monkland area are provided by a variety of operators, some of whom provide only a single service, often as a commuter link to Glasgow city centre. Many of the services identified mainly operated routes linking Coatbridge to surrounding towns such as Airdrie, Motherwell, Hamilton and Glasgow. The services operated by the smaller operators appear to target the individual communities (including Old Monkland) within the Coatbridge area. However, these services are limited, although valuable, in that they exist essentially to provide a service to those commuting to work in Glasgow. There is, however, a problem with public transport provision outside these peak periods.

There is no consistent fare structure for the services operating in the case study area. The information provided by the smaller transport operators show cheaper fares. The fares for the services operated by FirstGlasgow are similar to those described in the above section on Castlemilk (a 'First Value' ticket offers an off peak adult day return for £1.50 which is valid for travel city-wide, after 9.30am, Monday to Friday: the same ticket, but for travel network-wide, costs £1.90), although an off-peak return fare within Lanarkshire is £1.50 and between Lanarkshire and Glasgow is £1.90. The Dial-a-Bus community transport scheme operated by SPT is available, subject to the same entry criteria as that described in the section on Castlemilk. The service costs £0.40 per single journey for concession card holders and £0.60 for non-concession card holders. No other community transport schemes were identified in the area (Hine and Mitchell, 2001).

Policy Context

The North Lanarkshire Council envisages an inclusive society where there is equal access to opportunities, facilities and resources and individuals participate in shaping the policies affecting them. By promoting social inclusion there is recognition of the need to promote access for all. This includes the promotion of access on foot and by bicycle, encouraging the use of bus and rail services, access for road users, traffic management, and involvement in decision-making and coordinated action. There is, however, recognition that creating a totally barrier-free environment is unlikely to be a practical proposition, as the needs of different groups will inevitably result in competition for resources and space.

However, the council have identified that future priorities should include the creation of more equitable access, giving preference to those who are most disadvantaged by the existing built environment and current land use and travel patterns. There is recognition that this must be promoted in balance while supporting the economic role of transport. The key objective presented in the strategy is the creation of an integrated walking, cycling and public transport network which can match the access advantages offered by the private car. Delivering this network meets the needs of the whole population, and supports the health and prosperity aims. The strategy outlines policies to increase access on foot and by bicycle and to improve services, vehicles and infrastructure in order to make public transport more appealing and accessible.

Three Areas Compared

A household survey was undertaken in each of the areas discussed in this chapter. The purpose of the survey was to collect data that would be used to examine context-specific relationships and the experiences of different groups quantitatively.[6] The data collected provide insights into the nature of transport disadvantage in these areas. The questionnaire also collected a wealth of information on individuals within these three areas that provides useful background information in terms of housing, family structure, income and education. This background information is discussed further in this chapter; the relationships between these variables and travel behaviour are explored in Chapter 4.

Household Structure and Tenure

The majority of households (26.7 per cent) in the study consisted of one person living alone. Twenty-four per cent of the sample consisted of households that can be described as two people living together, 9.5 per cent of households described themselves as a single parent household, 20.1 per cent as a couple with dependent children and 19.6 per cent described themselves as another type of group (either related or unrelated) living together. In Leith, most respondents described their household as single person (34 per cent) or as two people living together (26.6 per cent) (Table 3.2). The largest proportion of single parents resided within in Castlemilk (13.2 per cent). Household type is a significant determining factor (as is tenure) in explaining car access levels. Single person and single parent families rely on lifts or have no car access at all: 59.6 per cent of single person households and 61.5 per cent of single parent families rely on lifts from neighbours or other family members. Couples with or without children have higher levels of car access.

A significant relationship was found between household type and age, and gender.[7] In the majority of single parent families, the respondent was found to be female and within the 30–40 age group. Most female respondents lived in single person households. Single person households were dominated by those aged 40–60 and over 60 (Table 3.3).

The majority of households (51.1 per cent) stated that they normally lived in households with two adults. Sixty-two per cent of respondents also stated that they had no dependent children living in the household. Fifteen per cent and 13 per cent of respondents stated their households had one and two dependent children (aged under 16 in their household) respectively. In Leith

Table 3.2   Household type and case study area

Household type	Case study area			Total
	Leith	*Castlemilk*	*Coatbridge*	
One person living alone	34.0	22.9	22.8	26.7
Two people living together as a couple	26.6	21.2	24.4	24.1
A single parent family	5.3	13.4	10.0	9.5
A couple with dependent children	14.9	24.6	21.1	20.1
Another type group, either related or unrelated	19.1	17.9	21.7	19.6

Table 3.3   Household type and age

Household type	Age					Total
	Under 16	*16–30*	*30–40*	*40–60*	*Over 60*	
One person living alone	–	9.9	16.1	25.2	47.4	26.6
Two people living together as a couple	25.0	23.8	14.4	18.9	37.8	24.3
A single parent family	–	11.9	16.9	11.9	0.6	9.7
A couple with dependent children	25.0	19.8	41.5	22.0	1.3	19.9
Another type of group, either related or unrelated	50.0	34.7	11.0	22.0	12.8	19.5
Total (%)	0.7	18.8	21.9	29.6	29	100.0

the higher number of single adult households is noticeable. This is due to there being a much younger population in this area: 27 per cent are aged 16–30 compared to much lower proportions in Castlemilk (14 per cent) and Coatbridge (13 per cent). Leith and Coatbridge were also found to have the largest proportions of households with no children (39.9 per cent and 31 per cent respectively). More households in Castlemilk stated they had two or three children (41.1 per cent and 47.1 per cent) than in Leith and Coatbridge.

Overall, 55.6 per cent stated that they lived in flats, either in tenements or four in a block, while an additional 10.9 per cent inhabited a flat in a high rise block. Twenty-four per cent of respondents lived in a terraced house compared to 9.4 per cent who lived in a house or bungalow.[8] In Coatbridge, the highest proportion of respondents occupied a house: 22.5 per cent lived in a detached or semidetached house and 46.1 per cent lived in a terraced house. In Leith and Castlemilk this figure is much lower. The majority of people in these two areas resided in flats, while occupation of high rise flats was more prevalent in Leith. These differences are illustrated in Table 3.4.

Twenty-eight point five per cent of respondents stated that they were buying their accommodation with the help of a mortgage or loan. Twenty-four per cent stated that they rented from a local authority and 12.2 per cent stated that they rented from a local housing association. Eight per cent of people stated that they rented from a private landlord and a further 8 per cent stated that they lived rent free (this category included social security payments and rent free in a relative's or friend's property. When household accommodation is analysed by the tenure categories significant differences emerge.[9]

Table 3.4   Household accommodation of respondents

Accommodation		Case study area			Total
		Leith	*Castlemilk*	*Coatbridge*	
House or	Count	3	8	40	51
bungalow	% within case study area	1.6%	4.5%	22.5%	9.4%
House	Count	16	31	82	129
(terraced)	% within case study area	8.6%	17.6%	46.1%	23.9%
Flat (tenement or	Count	124	128	48	300
four-in-a-block)	% within case study area	66.7%	72.7%	27.0%	55.6%
Flat	Count	42	9	8	59
(high-rise block)	% within case study area	22.6%	5.1%	4.5%	10.9%
Other	Count	1	0	0	1
	% within case study area	0.5%	0	0	0.2%
Total	Count	186	176	178	540
	% within case study area	100%	100%	100%	100%

Significant differences between case study area by tenure category were also found to exist (Table 3.5). In Coatbridge, 39.4 per cent paid rent to a local authority compared to 12.8 per cent in Leith and 20.6 per cent in Castlemilk. Larger proportions in Leith and Castlemilk however paid rent to housing associations (11.2 per cent and 22.2 per cent) respectively compared to 3.3 per cent in Coatbridge. Seventy-five per cent of those paying rent to a private landlord resided in Leith. For those purchasing property with the help of a mortgage or loan, the highest proportion resided in Leith (37.1 per cent),

Table 3.5　Tenure by case study area, % of respondents

Tenure	Case study area			Total
	Leith	*Castlemilk*	*Coatbridge*	
Pay rent – local authority	12.8	20.6	39.4	24.1
Pay rent – housing association	11.2	22.2	3.3	12.2
Pay rent – private landlord	17.6	3.9	2.2	8.0
Own outright	22.9	14.4	16.7	18.1
Buying with the help of a mortgage or loan	30.9	26.7	27.8	28.5
Live rent free	4.8	11.7	8.9	8.4
Other	0	0.6	1.7	0.7

although it was evenly spread with 32.1 per cent in Coatbridge and 30.8 per cent in Castlemilk.

Tenure was found to have a significant impact on levels of access to a car. Regular car access is associated with home ownership. This is reported in more detail in Chapter 4.

Health and Mobility

Health can have a significant impact on access to transport. Despite 81 per cent of respondents stating that their health had been good or fairly good, significant minorities of those interviewed had specific problems. Proportions of those stating that they had health problems were highest for the response 'problems or a disability connected with arms, legs, hands, feet, back or neck' at 28.3 per cent (n=156) and 'chest/breathing problems, asthma, bronchitis' at 21.4 per cent (n=118). Problems associated with vision and hearing accounted for 12.7 per cent and 10.7 per cent respectively of the total number of respondents.

A large proportion of respondents stated that they could walk unaided for over half a mile (83.3 per cent), while only 6.4 per cent stated that they could walk unaided for less than 100 yards. There was a high proportion of respondents who stated that they experienced no difficulty in undertaking a range of activities. For example, 79.2 per cent stated they had no problems 'climbing stairs' and 82.8 per cent stated that they had no difficulty 'walking for at least 10 minutes'. Some respondents, however, stated that they found difficulties with the following activities when accessing the public transport system:

- 5.7 per cent 'always' found difficulty in using a bus;
- 5.1 per cent 'sometimes' found difficulty in using a bus;
- 1.8 per cent 'always' had difficulty in using a taxi;
- 3.1 per cent 'sometimes' had difficulty in using a taxi;
- 2.8 per cent 'always' had difficulty using a train;
- 3.2 per cent 'sometimes' had difficulty using a car;
- 10.6 per cent 'always' had difficulty in walking for at least 10 minutes;
- 6.6 per cent 'sometimes' had difficulty in walking for at least 10 minutes;
- 10.4 per cent 'always' had difficulty in standing for at least 10 minutes;
- 6.8 per cent 'sometimes' had difficulty in standing for at least 10 minutes.

Neighbourhood

An overwhelming majority of the respondents stated that they liked living in their neighbourhood (90 per cent). This high level of satisfaction with the quality of the neighbourhood is also reflected in the large proportions of the sample that stated that they would wish to 'stay here' (55.9 per cent) or 'move within their neighbourhood' (14.9 per cent). Nevertheless, 29.2 per cent of all respondents stated that they would 'prefer to move to another area'.

The reasons given for preferring to move, either within the local area or to another area, were related either to the size or the nature of their house. For example, people wanted to move to a larger or smaller house, to a flat located on the ground floor, to a cheaper rent, to share with different people, or to a house with a garden. Many people also mentioned a wish to be closer to the city centre or to be able to access certain facilities more easily (a better library, better shops, university, or the workplace). Others expressed a wish to leave their local area as they felt it was bad or depressing. Table 3.6 shows the proportions citing health, personal reasons, improved housing/larger house, improve accessibility and poor environmental quality (including noise and neighbours) as reasons for leaving the neighbourhood. There is a difference between the case study areas in terms of these responses associated with preferring to move. In Castlemilk and Coatbridge, respondents are more likely to move due noise, neighbours and poorer environmental quality, whereas in Leith respondents indicated that they would prefer to move to improved housing.

Respondents were asked to rate on a five-point scale the degree to which they agreed with a range of statements. Most items were scored favourably, but things for young people to do, facilities for children and facilities for parking were areas perceived more negatively. Table 3.7 provides further information on the proportions agreeing and disagreeing with these statements.

Table 3.6   Reason for preferring to move (%) by case study area

	Leith *n=91*	Castlemilk *n=77*	Coatbridge *n=71*	Total
Improved transport links and accessibility	8.8	5.2	0	5.0
Poor health	4.4	6.5	5.6	5.4
Improved housing	40.7	23.4	32.4	32.6
Personal reasons	20.9	20.8	25.4	22.2
Noise, neighbours, poor environment	25.3	44.2	36.6	34.7

Table 3.7   'The neighbourhood you live in ...'

	Agree	Agree strongly	Neither agree nor disagree	Disagree strongly	Disagree
The neighbourhood you live in ...					
is well maintained and tidy	9.3	40.6	11.5	27.3	11.3
has *good* public transport	12.2	68.6	9.9	7.3	2.0
has plenty of open space	8.8	61.1	9.5	17.5	3.1
is a safe area	4.4	48.8	21.8	17.9	7.1
is quiet and not too noisy	7.8	54.7	13.3	16.8	7.3
has friendly people	14.8	67.5	12.6	3.5	1.6
has things for young people to do	2.4	20.6	23	39.6	14.4
has good local shops	7.1	62	10.2	16.4	4.2
has good leisure facilities	4.6	50.6	16.8	21.4	6.6
has good local schools	8.1	62.9	23.7	4.2	1.1
has good facilities for children	2.0	29.9	29	31.7	7.5
has facilities for parking	2.8	36.7	13.9	35.4	11.2

At a more disaggregated level there are some interesting differences between areas. Leith is regarded as less tidy and well maintained (37 per cent of respondents disagreed), compared to Castlemilk and Coatbridge, where people agreed that their areas were tidy and well maintained (42.5 per cent and 52.2 per cent of respondents respectively). In each area a high proportion of the respondents stated that their area did not have good facilities for children. In all areas, a significant proportion of the sample felt their area had good public transport: 61.9 per cent in Leith, 67.4 per cent in Castlemilk and 76.7 per cent in Coatbridge.

Neighbourhoods also exhibited a high concentration of friends and family nearby. Fifty point two per cent of respondents stated that most of their friends and relatives lived in a mixture of locations (i.e. another town or suburb, local neighbourhood) while 36.1 per cent stated that close friends and relatives lived in the local neighbourhood. Fifty-one point seven per cent of respondents stated that they had up to four friends living within a mile of them. These local support networks also provided security in that substantial proportions of respondents stated that they could rely friends and family to help them with a variety of situations, including:

- 60.6 per cent of respondents stated that they would have someone to help them most or all of the time if they were confined to bed;
- 81.6 per cent of respondents stated that they would have someone to count on to listen to you when you needed to talk most or all of the time;
- 76.8 per cent of respondents stated that they would have someone who could give them good advice in a crisis most or all of the time;
- 77.8 per cent of respondents stated that they would have someone to take them to the doctors most or all of the time if they needed it;
- 73.3 per cent of respondents stated they would have someone to help them with their chores if they were sick most or all of the time.

Employment, Education and Training

Twenty-three per cent of respondents stated that their employment status was full-time employed, 10.5 per cent part-time employed, 27.7 per cent retired and 6.4 per cent described themselves as unemployed and seeking work. The proportions in full-time work are significantly lower than those recorded nationally. Those in part-time work, retired and the unemployed are prevalent in each of the case study areas.[10] These responses can be seen in Table 3.8.

As can be seen from Table 3.9, of those who were employed full-time a higher proportion (45.7 per cent) lived in Leith. However Leith also has a higher proportion of those unemployed and seeking work. A higher proportion (42.4 per cent) of those who were permanently retired lived in Coatbridge. Coatbridge also had the smallest proportion (26.1 per cent) of those who classified themselves as in full-time education. The majority of those who were looking after home or family resided in Castlemilk.

Women are more likely to be in part-time employment – 14.2 per cent compared to 4.4 per cent for men. Men, on the other hand, were more likely to be employed full time (35 per cent) compared to women (16.3 per cent).

Table 3.8   Employment status

Employment status	% *n=545*
Self-employed	3.1
Employed full-time	23.3
Employed part-time	10.5
Looking after the home or family	9.9
Permanently retired from work	27.7
Unemployed and seeking work	6.4
In full-time education school	1.8
In full-time education (further/higher)	4.2
Permanently sick or disabled	8.6
Unable to work because of short-term illness or injury	2.8
Other	1.7
Total	100

Table 3.9   Employment status and case study area

Employment status	Case study area		
	Leith	Castlemilk	Coatbridge
Self-employed	3.7	3.4	2.2
Employed full-time	30.9	15.8	22.8
Employed part-time	10.6	11.9	8.9
Looking after the home or family	6.9	13.0	10.0
Permanently retired from work	20.2	27.7	35.6
Unemployed and seeking work	8.0	5.6	5.6
In full-time education school	2.1	2.8	0.6
In full-time education (further/higher)	5.3	4.0	3.3
Permanently sick or disabled	8.5	11.3	6.1
Unable to work because of short-term illness or injury	1.6	2.8	3.9
Other	3.1	1.7	1.1
Total	100%	100%	100%

Table 3.10 Employment status and gender

Employment status	Male	Female	Total
Self-employed	4.4%	2.4%	3.1%
Employed full-time	35.0%	16.3%	23.3%
Employed part-time	4.4%	14.2%	10.5%
Looking after the home or family	2.4%	14.5%	9.9%
Permanently retired from work	25.7%	28.7%	27.6%
unemployed and seeking work	8.7%	5.0%	6.4%
In full-time education (school)	1.0%	2.4%	1.8%
In full-time education (further/higher)	4.9%	3.8%	4.2%
Permanently sick or disabled	10.7%	7.4%	8.6%
Unable to work because of short-term illness or injury	2.4%	3.0%	2.8%

Household Income and Expenditure Patterns

Forty-eight point five per cent of households in this study had gross household incomes of under £200 per week (annual gross household income of £7,800–£10,300). The average gross household income figure for Scotland is £367.40 (1996/97 prices). Comparisons across the three areas indicate that a greater proportion of respondents in Castlemilk have household incomes at this level compared to the other two areas in the study: 56.9 per cent on a gross weekly household income of under £200 compared to 41.5 per cent in Leith and 48.8 per cent in Coatbridge (Table 3.11).[11]

Households with gross annual incomes below £10,300 are more likely to be one person living alone, single parent family and another type of grouping. Households earning in excess of £10,300 per year were more likely to be two people living together as a couple and couple with dependent children (Table 3.12). Household expenditure on different items was also examined. On rent and mortgage payments, the largest proportion (33 per cent) of respondents spent nothing, 13.6 per cent spent £40–50 and 10.7 per cent spent £50–59. On food and groceries, the largest proportion (19.1 per cent) of respondents spent £30–39 and 15 per cent spent £40–49. On bills, 21 per cent of people spent £10–19 and 19.9 per cent spent £20–29. On eating out or buying takeaway food, the overwhelming majority spent very little: 41.2 per cent spent nothing, 18.1 per cent spent under £10 and 17.4 per cent spent £10–19. This was similar to the spending on leisure activities, where 34.9 per cent of respondents spent nothing, 23.3 per cent spent under £10 and 14.8 spent £10–19 (Table 3.13).

Table 3.11   Household income by case study area, % of respondents in case study area

Household income per year	per week	Leith	Castlemilk	Coatbridge	Total
Under £2,600	Under £50	2.8	0.7	1.3	1.7
£2,600–£3,800	£50–£74	9.1	11.7	6.0	8.9
£3,900–£5,100	£75–£99	6.8	14.6	10.7	10.4
£5,200–£7,700	£100–£149	8.0	17.5	17.4	13.9
£7,800–£10,300	£150–£199	14.8	12.4	13.4	13.6
£10,400–£12,900	£200–£249	12.5	11.7	12.1	12.1
£13,000–£15,500	£250–£299	7.4	5.8	8.7	7.4
£15,600–£20,700	£300–£399	13.1	7.3	5.4	8.9
£20,800–£25,900	£400–£499	6.3	7.3	10.1	7.8
£26,000–£31,100	£500–£599	7.4	5.1	7.4	6.7
£31,200 or more	£600 or more	11.9	5.8	7.4	8.7

The spending on transport was a little higher, with 40 per cent of respondents spending under £10 and 22.6 per cent spending £10–19. Nine per cent of respondents spent nothing on transport.

The effect of gross household income on all of these items of household expenditure is marked and statistically significant. Forty-four per cent of those on an income below £10,300 paid nothing in rent or mortgage payments. Sixty-two per cent of those on incomes under £10,300 spend up to £39 per week on groceries and food, compared to only 27.7 per cent of those on incomes over £10,300. Similarly, for telephone, electricity and gas bills, 70.3 per cent of those on annual incomes under £10,300 pay up to £29 per week on bills compared to 47.1 per cent in the higher income band. Lower income groups also tend not engage in leisure activities (eating out, entertainment, hobbies, takeaway food). Fifty-seven point six per cent of those on household incomes under £10,300 spent nothing on eating out or takeaway food and 74 per cent within the same income banding spent nothing or up to £10 per week on other types of leisure activities. For transport expenses (bus fares, taxi fares and petrol) lower income groups also tended to spend less. Twelve point eight per cent of those households on incomes up to £10,300 per year spent nothing on transport, while 57.1 per cent spend under £10. Fifty-nine point three per cent of those households earning more than £10,300 per year spent £10–£39 on travel (Table 3.14). Those on lower incomes also worry more about money (Table 3.15).

Table 3.12 Percentage of respondents by household type within household income

Gross annual household income	One person living alone	Two people living together as a couple	A single parent family	A couple with dependent children	Another type of group, related or unrelated	No.
<£10,300	34.8	18.8	16.5	10.7	19.2	224
>£10,300	16.6	29.4	3.8	31.1	19.1	235

Table 3.13 Household spending on different items, % of respondents

Spending in a week	On rent and mortgage payments	On food and groceries	Bills – telephone, electricity and gas	Eating out or buying takeaway food	Leisure activities, entertainment and hobbies	Transport – bus/rail/taxi fares, petrol
Nothing	33.3	1.4	8.5	41.2	34.9	9.1
Under £10	3.1	2.7	9.2	18.1	23.3	40.0
£10–19	4.6	6.4	21.0	17.4	14.8	22.6
£20–29	4.4	13.8	19.9	9.5	11.6	13.2
£30–39	6.3	19.1	12.2	6.9	6.7	8.9
£40–49	13.6	15.0	10.6	2.3	4.2	2.8
£50–59	10.7	12.7	6.5	2.1	1.9	1.2
£60–79	6.8	12.5	3.2	1.9	1.0	1.2
£80–99	4.6	6.4	2.3	0.2	0.6	0.6
£100–119	5.0	6.2	2.1	0.0	0.4	0.2
£120–139	2.6	1.4	0.9	0.2	0.4	0.0
£140–159	0.4	0.8	0.7	0.2	0.2	0.0
£160 or over	4.6	1.6	2.8	0.0	0.0	0.0

Table 3.14   Spending on transport and household income

Transport – bus/rail/taxi fares, petrol	Household income Less than £10,300	More than £10,300	Total
Nothing	12.8%	4.2%	8.4%
Under £10	57.1%	25.4%	40.7%
£10–19	17.4%	27.1%	22.4%
£20–29	10.0%	16.5%	13.4%
£30–39	1.8%	15.7%	9.0%
£40–49	.9%	4.7%	2.9%
£50–59		2.5%	1.3%
£60–79		2.1%	1.1%
£80–99		1.3%	.7%
£100–119		.4%	.2%
Total	100.0%	100.0%	100.0%

Table 3.15   Worried about money by gross annual household income

Worried about money	Household income Less than £10,300	More than £10,300
Almost all the time	27.7%	19.9%
Quite often	15.5%	12.7%
Only sometimes	21.4%	18.2%
Never	35.0%	49.2%
Refused	.5%	0.0%
Count	220	236
% of total	48.2%	51.8%

Conclusion

In Edinburgh, Glasgow and North Lanarkshire there is a recognised and stated policy requirement to address issues of social exclusion and the linkages with transport. Edinburgh has been more radical in its approach to investigating these issues. This may reflect the degree of cross-disciplinary working within the City of Edinburgh local authority and also that they are the planning, highways and transport authority. Glasgow and North Lanarkshire authorities are highways and planning authorities, with the transport function being exercised by Strathclyde Passenger Transport. This division of responsibility obviously makes it more difficult for organisations to match the level of cross-departmental working that has been achieved in Edinburgh.

Leith, the historic port area within the City of Edinburgh, has experienced rapid change through regeneration of the area. The population is younger, more people are single and own their accommodation or are buying it with the assistance of a mortgage. Symptomatic of this rapid change, a larger proportion of people living within the area were found to have higher incomes (£15,600–£20,700) and lower incomes (under £2,600) than the other two areas examined in this book. In comparison, Castlemilk, a peripheral housing estate in Glasgow, and Coatbridge, a freestanding town in North Lanarkshire, are markedly different. Their populations tend to be older with larger proportions living as a couple with or without children. In Coatbridge there is more house or bungalow accommodation than in Leith and Castlemilk, where the housing stock is characterised by high rise or tenemental flatted accommodation. Public sector housing is more prevalent in Castlemilk and Coatbridge but significant proportions were also found to be buying their homes in these areas.

Tenure has a significant impact on levels of access to a car – in fact, it is a proxy measure of household income. Regular access to a car is to be found amongst those households where the home is owned outright or where the home is being bought with the help of a mortgage or loan. Households consisting of two people living together or couples with dependent children also experienced high levels of car access.

Despite differences in tenure, income and population characteristics there was a high level of satisfaction with the quality of the neighbourhood. In each case respondents' neighbourhoods exhibited high concentrations of friends and family living nearby. These local support networks clearly provide security in that substantial proportions of respondents stated that they could rely on family and friends to help them at a time of crisis or when they were sick.

The review of this data on population characteristics and the nature of these neighbourhoods has suggested that in these areas policy objectives of modal shift are not appropriate in locations where there is likely to be little modal shift. As we shall see in Chapter 4, in Leith and Castlemilk walking and bus-based public transport account for a significant share of journeys compared to car. In Coatbridge the picture is somewhat different. As in 1991 the car dominates many journeys made in this area.

Notes

1   Within these areas individual electoral wards were chosen for the purposes of the survey administration. A fuller description of the survey methodology is available in the appendix to this volume.
2   See appendix for information on bus services and typical frequencies.
3   The Castlemilk Umbrella Group was formed 11 years ago and is made up of community organisations and projects who represent a variety of interests and who deal with issues throughout Castlemilk. Cited here are transport issues identified by the group.
4   See appendix.
5   This information was provided by North Lanarkshire Council and the details are taken from an internal document provided by the Council.
6   The data that were collected also provide primary evidence on the nature of transport disadvantage in these three areas. The sampling strategy was based on a quota method in a bid to be representative of the population in each of the case study areas. The proportion of households within each case study area who had a 'motor vehicle' was higher than intended. This is less problematic than it might appear in terms of being representative of the three populations. The 1991 census, on which the quota sample for each area was based, is outdated and the number of households who own a car is thought to have increased in each area since 1991. For this study a significant proportion of the sample in each area does not own a vehicle and experiences differential levels of access to the car.
7   Details of age and sex distributions in each case study area can be found in the appendix.
8   The Scottish Household Survey (Scottish Executive, 2000) respondents were asked to describe their household accommodation – 62.5 per cent described it as a house or bungalow, 36.7 per cent described it as a flat (including four-in-a-block) if it is detached (30.1 per cent), semidetached (35.2 per cent) and terraced (34.8 per cent).
9   SHS (Scottish Executive, 2000) found that 22.2 per cent owned their accommodation outright, 37.9 per cent were buying it with the help of a mortgage or loan, 0.7 per cent were part rent/part buy, 37.5 per cent were renting, and 1.2 per cent living rent free.
10 SHS found 4.1 per cent self-employed, 29.2 per cent full-time employed, 8.5 per cent part-time employed, 6.8 per cent looking after home/family, 17.3 per cent permanently retired from work, 3.4 per cent unemployed and seeking work, 15.7 per cent at school, 3.5 per cent in higher/further education, 0.3 per cent in government work/training scheme, 3.9 per cent permanently sick or disabled, 0.6 per cent unable to work due to short-term illness, 6.1 per cent preschool and 0.7 other (Scottish Executive, 2000).
11 In 2000 the poverty lines before housing costs and for net incomes (after tax) were £103 per week for a single adult, £170 per week for a couple with no children, and for a couple with three children aged under 12, £281 per week (www.lowpayunit.org.uk/research/lines.shtml).

Chapter 4

Transport Choices and Disadvantage

Introduction

The differences in the location of each neighbourhood, population structure in terms of age and gender, the type of housing available and tenure, employment status and levels of unemployment, and income will have an effect on the amount and type of transport available. This chapter examines the nature of the transport choices available to people residing in Castlemilk, Coatbridge and Leith – the three case study areas for this work. Previous work has highlighted levels of differential access between different age groups, genders and income groups (Grayling, 2001; RCEP, 1995; Hamilton et al., 2000). This evidence is supported by the experiences of those residing in these three areas. This chapter addresses these issues in terms of access to a car and public transport use. The previous chapter presented information on the characteristics of the population in these three areas. This chapter concerns itself solely with transport choice.

Those most likely to experience transport disadvantage are those on low incomes, women, the elderly and disabled people and children (Hine and Mitchell, 2001; DETR, 2000). Essentially, these groups are those with traditionally lower levels of access to cars and this is at a period in time when the car is not only the dominant mode for all journeys over one mile but also plays a significant role in journeys under one mile as well (DETR, 1998; RCEP, 1994). This is despite evidence from the NTS for the UK that suggests that availability of bus services has changed little over the period 1985/86 to 1995/97. In 1995/97 87 per cent of households lived within a six minutes of a bus stop, compared to 86 per cent in 1985/86 (DETR, 1998).

We have seen in Chapter 1 that the very nature of transport disadvantage and social exclusion raises questions of not only the ways in which transport policy should be delivered but also the types of interventions that can be used to ameliorate the effect of social exclusion. The paradox here is that although this is seen to be an important policy area, the major policy interventions have been shaped around the desire to encourage a modal shift from the private car to public transport, cycling and walking. Although improvements to public transport services can benefit non-car users and the socially excluded, there are issues about how services can best be structured to alleviate exclusion and encourage participation from those groups that have historically felt the consequences of transport disadvantage.

Car Access

Licence Holding

Overall 40.8 per cent of respondents held a full driving licence and 12.3 per cent a provisional driving licence. A higher proportion of those who currently hold a full driving licence reside in Leith (38.1 per cent) than in Castlemilk (26.5 per cent) or Coatbridge (35.4 per cent). Forty-two point five per cent of those surveyed had never held a UK driving licence. The proportions who have not held a licence were found to be similar in each area Leith (31 per cent), Castlemilk (34.1 per cent) and Coatbridge (34.9 per cent). The most marked difference in those that have never held a driving licence is in terms of gender – 77.8 per cent of those who have never held a licence are female. This is also the case for those who currently hold a provisional licence – 70.1 per cent are female. Analysis of the data also showed that 1.1 per cent are currently disqualified from driving and 3.3 per cent have had their licence suspended on medical grounds.[1]

In addition to gender, age has a significant impact on the ability to hold a driving licence. The majority of those holding a provisional licence are in the aged 16 to 30 years, whereas the majority of those currently disqualified from driving (50 per cent) and for those with their licence suspended on medical grounds (50 per cent) are in the aged 60 and over (Table 4.1).

Income is also a powerful determinant of car access. As the income increases so does car ownership. Those who had access to a car through their employment were concentrated in the higher income brackets – in the main, those with a household income of £13,000 and above. Table 4.2 shows clearly that income can have an impact on licence holding ability. Those on lower incomes are more likely to have their licence suspended on medical grounds, it is possible that this is a proxy for those on lower incomes having poorer health. Those on lower incomes are less likely to have a full driving licence than those on higher incomes, and are more likely to have never held a UK driving licence.

Those who have 'never held a UK driving licence' were also asked the reasons for not learning to drive. Reasons given ranged from concerns over

Table 4.1   Age and licence holding

	Under 16	16 to 30	30–40	40–60	Over 60
		Age in years (in bands)			
Currently hold a full driving licence	–	14.9%	28.5%	34.4%	22.2%
Currently hold a provisional licence	–	39.4%	27.3%	24.2%	9.1%
Never held a UK driving licence	1.8%	16.8%	15.0%	27.4%	38.9%
Currently disqualified from driving	–	16.7%	16.7%	16.7%	50.0%
Licence suspended on medical grounds	–	11.1%	16.7%	22.2%	50.0%

Table 4.2   Household income and driving licence

	Under £7,700	£7,800–£15,500	£15,600 or more
	Household income (recoded)		
Currently hold a full driving licence	19.1%	33.2%	47.7%
Currently hold a provisional licence	28.6%	44.6%	26.8%
Never held a UK driving licence	49.5%	31.0%	19.6%
Currently disqualified from driving	25.0%	50.0%	25.0%
Licence suspended on medical grounds	81.3%	18.8%	–
	34.6%	33.3%	32.0%

the cost of learning to drive, as well the cost of running a car, to psychological barriers such as not having the confidence to learn to drive. Others said they had never seen the need to learn as there was always someone else within the household who did drive. Some never felt the need as they preferred public transport or walking.

Those who had a licence (i.e. those who currently hold a full driving licence and those who hold a provisional licence) were asked how often they drove. Tables 4.3 shows how often respondents who had a licence reported that they drove.[2] The most notable differences between case study areas is the higher proportion of drivers within Coatbridge (49.1 per cent) who drive every day. Whereas the highest proportion (33.7 per cent) of respondents who never drive reside within Castlemilk.

Table 4.3   Frequency of driving

| How often do you drive? | Case study area | | | Total |
	Leith	Castlemilk	Coatbridge	
Every day	25.5%	37.0%	49.1%	37.3%
At least three times a week	11.3%	9.8%	3.7%	8.2%
Once or twice a week	14.2%	12.0%	9.3%	11.8%
At least 2 or 3 times a month	1.9%	1.1%	1.9%	1.6%
At least once a month	2.8%	1.1%	1.9%	2.0%
Less than once a month	20.8%	5.4%	3.7%	10.1%
Never	23.6%	33.7%	30.6%	29.1%

Vehicle Ownership and Availability

Respondents were asked questions about their access to a vehicle. Overall, 55.6 per cent of respondents said that they had a motor vehicle available for private use by them or a member of their household. Of these respondents, the majority stated that they had only one vehicle available to them (67.8 per cent), while around one-fifth (22.6 per cent) stated that they had two vehicles available to them.[3]

It is clear that differential access to vehicles is an issue of major importance. Although 25.6 per cent stated that they own their own car/van, significant proportions also relied lifts from within the household (13.6 per cent) or from friends, neighbours or relatives (36 per cent) whenever they were needed or sometimes (Table 4.4). Twenty-nine per cent of respondents in Coatbridge stated that they owned a car or van compared to 24.6 per cent in Castlemilk and 23.1 per cent in Leith. In Leith, a higher proportion (14 per cent) of respondents stated that they never have access to a car/van compared to 9.1 per cent in Castlemilk and 7.7 per cent in Coatbridge. Car use is least in Leith and most in Coatbridge (Table 4.4).

Further analysis of car access in terms of 'regular car access' (i.e. owning their own vehicle), 'sporadic access to a car' (i.e. through lifts from another household member and friends), and 'no access at all' revealed a statistically significant relationship between gender and car access. Men were more likely to have regular access to a car than women were (Table 4.5). Women were more likely to rely on lifts or have no access at all. Similarly those on higher income (over £15,600) were more likely to have regular access to a car than those on lower incomes (under £7,700 and between £7,800–15,500) who were more likely to have no access at all and only some access through lifts from friends, respectively (Table 4.6). Women and those on lower incomes clearly experience lower levels of access to the car than men and those on higher incomes.

Housing tenure also has a significant impact on determining levels of car access. Regular car access is associated with home ownership – that is where a home is owned outright or where the home is being bought with the help of a mortgage or loan. In comparison a large proportion of those relying on lifts live in rented sector accommodation. Sporadic car access is associated with these tenure groups (Table 4.7).

Car Use and Expenditure on Travel

Non-ownership of a car has serious implications for the amount of times during a week or month that you are able to visit certain types of facilities. If access to a vehicle was more readily available this would seemingly have little impact on certain types of trips, for example journeys to the bank, public house, library and church. However, trips to the supermarket, sports/leisure facilities and the cinema would increase (Table 4.8).

The majority (74.5 per cent) of those respondents who owned a car had had it for over five years, while 18.3 per cent had had a car for one to five years and 7.2 per cent had had a car for less than a year. The main reasons given for buying a car were 'convenience', a need for a car due to work, and in some cases because there was no alternative (i.e. inadequately served by the public transport network).

On average, these respondents drove 11,644 miles in a year and the average fuel expenditure for the past week was £21.99. The minimum spent (in the last week) was nothing and the maximum was £75.00. Further analysis indicated that household income is a significant determinant of fuel expenditure. For those respondents on incomes of up to £7,700 per year and £7,800 to £15,500 per year most spent up to £15 per week. Respondents on higher incomes were more likely to spend between £15–£30 per week and over £30 per week on fuel (Table 4.9).

Table 4.4 Access to car, availability and case study area

Access to car	Case study area			Total
	Leith	Castlemilk	Coatbridge	
I own my own car/van	23.1%	24.6%	29.0%	25.6%
Access to a car/van owned by work – can use for personal use	5.4%	.6%	1.6%	2.6%
I own a motorbike or moped	3.2%	.6%	1.1%	1.7%
Access to a car owned by my work, but not for personal use	2.2%	–	1.1%	1.1%
Someone in my household owns a car/van which I can drive	3.2%	6.3%	4.4%	4.6%
Someone in household own car/van – lifts whenever needed	7.5%	10.9%	12.6%	10.3%
Someone in household owns car/van – provides lifts sometimes	2.7%	4.0%	3.3%	3.3%
A friend etc. owns car/van which I can drive	5.4%	2.9%	5.5%	4.6%
A friend etc. owns car/van – lifts whenever needed	17.2%	21.7%	18.6%	19.1%
A friend etc. owns car/van – provides lifts sometimes	16.1%	19.4%	15.3%	16.9%
I never have access to a car/van	14.0%	9.1%	7.7%	10.3%

Table 4.5 Car access and gender

Gender	Car access		No access at all	Total
	Regular car access	Relying on lifts		
Male	53.1%	24.6%	37.5%	37.1%
Female	46.9%	75.4%	62.5%	62.9%

Table 4.6   Car access and household income

Household income	Car access			Total
	Regular car access	*Relying on lifts*	*No access at all*	
Under £7,700	16.7%	46.3%	53.2%	34.7%
£7,800–15,500	31.7%	36.0%	27.7%	33.3%
£15,600 or more	51.6%	17.8%	19.1%	32.0%
Total	100.0%	100.0%	100.0%	100.0%

Table 4.7   Tenure and car access

Tenure	Car access			Total
	Regular car access	*Relying on lifts*	*No access at all*	
Pay rent –local authority	13.5%	32.5%	21.8%	23.9%
Pay rent – housing association	5.3%	14.9%	25.5%	12.2%
Pay rent – landlord	6.3%	7.8%	10.9%	7.5%
Own it outright	21.6%	16.0%	16.4%	18.3%
Buying with help of mortgage or loan	47.1%	16.8%	16.4%	28.6%
Live here rent free	5.8%	10.8%	9.1%	8.7%
Other	0.5%	1.1%	0.0%	0.8%

Twelve per cent of respondents indicated that they had sold or disposed of a vehicle without replacing it within the last five years. The majority (53.8 per cent) of those respondents were from Leith and the main reasons given were that it was too costly or for other reasons that were not defined. The larger proportions of those respondents stating that they had disposed of a motor vehicle were aged 30–40 (25 per cent) and 40–60 (34.4 per cent).

Travel to Work

Overall, the journey to work consisted of only one stage (88.1 per cent, n=170) indicating a reliance on modes that can access goods and services directly in each case study area. Travel to work in each case study area was markedly different in several respects (Table 4.10). In Leith, driving to work was less important than taking the bus, whereas in the other two case study areas driving

Table 4.8   Would a car change the amount of trips you made?

No, stay the same, going to ...	Regular car access	Relying on lifts	No access at all
Supermarket	59.6	56.9	58.2
Bank	84.2	83.0	87.3
Sports/leisure	60.7	75.5	67.3
Cinema	66.7	66.2	63.6
Pub	93.0	95.1	90.9
Library	89.5	82.0	88.9
Church	94.6	85.8	83.3
Yes, visit more ...			
Supermarket	38.6	38.2	38.2
Bank	14.0	16.2	12.7
Sports/leisure	39.3	23.7	32.7
Cinema	33.3	33.1	34.5
Pub	1.8	4.2	9.1
Library	10.5	17.2	9.3
Church	5.4	13.9	16.7

Table 4.9   Annual household income and fuel expenditure per week, % of households

	Up to £7, 700	£7,800– £15,500	£15,600 and over	Total
Up to £15	56.3	65.9	33.3	46.8
£15–£30	37.5	24.4	56.5	43.7
£30+	6.3	9.8	10.1	9.5
Total	100.0	100.0	100.0	100.0

was as important or more so than taking the bus. This is especially the case in Coatbridge. In each area walking played a significant role.

Further analysis revealed a significant relationship between mode used to travel to work and household income level. As indicated earlier in this chapter, driving becomes a more important mode of transport as income increases, whereas lower income groups are more likely to rely on the bus and less likely to walk to work (Table 4.11).

Table 4.10 Travel to work and case study area

Travel to work	Case study area			Total
	Leith	*Castlemilk*	*Coatbridge*	
Walking	16.3%	14.3%	16.4%	15.8%
Driving (car/van)	20.9%	35.7%	39.3%	30.5%
Passenger (car/van)	3.5%	5.4%	19.7%	8.9%
Bicycle	10.5%	–	–	4.4%
Works bus	4.7%	–	4.9%	3.4%
Ordinary service bus	38.4%	37.5%	6.6%	28.6%
Taxi/minicab	–	1.8%	6.6%	2.5%
Rail	–	–	4.9%	1.5%
Other	5.8%	5.4%	1.6%	4.4%
Total	100.0%	100.0%	100.0%	100.0%

Table 4.11 Household income and mode choice for travel to work

Mode	Household income			Total
	Under £7,700	*£7,800–£15,500*	*£15,600 or more*	
Walking	–	26.2%	11.6%	15.8%
Driving (car/van)	–	24.6%	37.5%	31.0%
Passenger (car/van)	–	13.1%	7.1%	8.7%
Bicycle	9.1%	–	7.1%	4.9%
Works bus	9.1%	3.3%	3.6%	3.8%
Ordinary service bus	63.6%	26.2%	25.9%	28.3%
Taxi/minicab	9.1%	3.3%	0.9%	2.2%
Rail	–	–	1.8%	1.1%
Other	9.1%	3.3%	4.5%	4.3%

For those in employment (full, part-time and looking after family), 14.5 per cent (n=46) stated that transport considerations had prevented them from looking for a job and 10.4 per cent (n=33) had stated that transport considerations had prevented them accepting a job offer. 43.4 per cent (n=20) stated that they had been continuously unemployed or not in paid work for over two years. Of this small number, the majority felt that transport considerations had prevented them from looking for work (n=10) and accepting a job (n=14). Travel to school/college/university was undertaken principally on foot (39.4 per cent), bus (33.3 per cent) and driving (15.2 per cent). Again, small numbers responded to questions surrounding transport considerations and the lack of access to jobs and education. The largest number of responses were related to prevented from looking for a job (n=7) (Table 4.12).

Use of Bus-based Public Transport

Accessibility of Bus Stops

Seventy-two per cent of respondents stated that the nearest bus stop to where they lived was less than three minutes away and 23.6 per cent stated that their bus stop was between three and six minutes' walk away (Table 4.13). These figures are comparable to those documenting the time taken to reach the bus stop that respondents used most often: 61.1 per cent stated that time taken by respondents to get to the bus stop most often used was less than three minutes walk away and 26.7 per cent stated between three and six minutes walk away. There were little differences between the case study areas in the general pattern of responses although there was a higher proportion (74.7 per cent) of respondents in Coatbridge within three minutes walk of the bus stop they used most often (Table 4.14). Overall three per cent of all respondents stated that never used the bus when asked about the bus stop they use most often.[4]

Perceived Service Frequency and Use of Services

Respondents were also asked to state the number of services that ran from their nearest bus stop: 48.1 per cent of respondents stated that they had up to two services running from their nearest bus stop. Respondents stated an average of 3.59 services (the standard deviation was 2.92). In addition to the number of services, respondents were asked to describe the frequency of the service that they use most often at different times of the day and were given the options of: at least one bus every ten minutes, a bus every 11–20 minutes, a bus every 21–30 minutes, a bus every 31–60 minutes, less frequent than one bus an hour, and no service. Table 4.15 shows the responses given in regarding the different times of day.

Thirty-nine point three per cent of respondents stated that the bus service/route that they used most often ran 'at least one bus every 10 minutes' during the day Monday to Friday. A larger proportion of respondents in Castlemilk (47.0 per cent) saw their service operating at least once every 10 minutes than Leith (32.4 per cent) and Coatbridge (39.4 per cent). However, more people

Table 4.12   Transport considerations and failure to access jobs, education or training

Transport considerations …	% employed	No.	% unemployed, looking after family or unable to work	No.	% education or training scheme	No.
prevented you from looking for a job	14.5	46	25	10	21.2	7
prevented you from accepting a job offer	10.4	33	35.9	14	12.1	4
prevented you from changing jobs	10.4	33	20.5	8	9.1	3
required you to change your job	1.9	6	12.8	5	6.1	2
required you to leave paid employment	1.9	6	15.4	6	0	0
required you to work fewer hours	4.1	13	7.7	3	9.1	3
prevented you from taking up any form of education or training	6.0	19	12.8	5	3.0	1

Table 4.13   Time to nearest bus stop

Time to nearest bus stop	Case study area			Total
	Leith	Castlemilk	Coatbridge	
Less than three minutes walk	75.5%	59.4%	79.9%	71.7%
Between 3 and 6 minutes walk	21.3%	33.9%	15.6%	23.6%
Six to 10 minutes walk	3.2%	6.1%	2.8%	4.0%
More than 10 minutes walk	0.0%	0.6%	1.7%	0.7%

Table 4.14 Time to bus stop used most often

Time to bus stop used most often

	Leith	Case study area Castlemilk	Coatbridge	Total
Less than 3 minutes walk	55.6%	53.6%	74.7%	61.1%
Between 3 and 6 minutes walk	31.0%	33.5%	14.9%	26.7%
6–10 minutes walk	9.6%	7.3%	2.9%	6.7%
More than 10 minutes walk	2.1%	2.2%	2.9%	2.4%
Never use the bus	1.6%	3.4%	4.6%	3.1%

Table 4.15 Frequency of local bus service

	% of respondents					
	At least one bus every 10 minutes	A bus every 11–20 minutes	A bus every 21–30 minutes	A bus every 31–60 minutes	Less frequent than one bus an hour	No service
During the day (Mondays–Fridays)	39.3	46.0	13.8	0.8	0.0	0.0
Evenings(Monday –Fridays)	7.6	23.5	31.8	13.1	1.9	22.1
Saturday	28.1	37.5	23.1	9.0	1.6	0.7
Sunday	1.0	11.2	28.0	29.5	9.9	20.3

in Leith (59.5 per cent) stated there was a bus every 11–20 minutes than respondents in Castlemilk (38.6 per cent) and Coatbridge (38.1 per cent). In the evenings (Monday–Friday) the majority of respondents stated there was one bus every 21–30 minutes. This mirrored the results within Castlemilk and Leith, although in Coatbridge an overwhelming majority (73 per cent) stated there was no service. A bus every 11–21 minutes was the most common response (37.5 per cent) regarding Saturday across the whole sample; however, within each case study area 'at least one bus every 10 minutes' was the most common response in Castlemilk and Coatbridge. On a Sunday 'a bus every 31–60 minutes' (29.5 per cent) or 'no service' (20.3 per cent) were more common responses. Although within Castlemilk (34.8 per cent) and Leith (40 per cent) the majority of respondents chose the response 'a bus every 21–30 minutes', in Coatbridge, 60.3 per cent stated there was no service on a Sunday.

Overall, 20.7 per cent of respondents stated that they used the bus every day and 14.2 per cent stated that they used the local bus service almost every day. These proportions were higher in Leith and Castlemilk, where 33.5 per cent and 22.8 per cent of respondents stated they used the bus every day. In Coatbridge, only 5.5 per cent stated that they used the bus every day. A higher proportion (28 per cent) of respondents in Coatbridge stated that they never used the bus compared to Leith (6.4 per cent) and Castlemilk (9.4 per cent). These differences are illustrated in Table 4.16.

Table 4.16   Frequency of use of local bus service within case study area

How often do you use the local bus service?	Leith	Castlemilk	Coatbridge	Total
		Case study area		*Total*
Every day	33.5%	22.8%	5.5%	20.7%
Almost every day	13.3%	15.0%	14.3%	14.2%
2 or 3 times a week	24.5%	23.3%	24.7%	24.2%
Once a week	7.4%	8.9%	8.2%	8.2%
Once a fortnight	3.2%	3.3%	2.2%	2.9%
Once a month	4.8%	3.3%	4.9%	4.4%
Very rarely	6.9%	13.9%	12.1%	10.9%
Never	6.4%	9.4%	28.0%	14.5%
Total	100%	100%	100%	100%

Further analysis also revealed significant differences between car access and frequency of bus use. Regular car access clearly results in lower levels of bus use or no use of local services. Eleven point six per cent of respondents who stated that they has regular car access also stated that they used the bus every day, compared to 32.1 per cent who used the bus regularly but who had no access at all to a car (Table 4.17).

Table 4.17 Car access and frequency of bus use

How often do you use the local bus service?	Car access Regular car access	Relying on lifts	No access at all	Total
Every day	11.6%	24.1%	32.1%	20.1%
Almost every day	8.2%	18.5%	17.9%	14.4%
2 or 3 times a week	16.9%	29.3%	26.8%	24.2%
Once a week	8.2%	9.3%	3.6%	8.3%
Once a fortnight	3.9%	2.6%	–	2.8%
Once a month	6.3%	3.0%	5.4%	4.5%
Very rarely	16.9%	7.4%	7.1%	11.1%
Never	28%	5.9%	7.1%	14.6%
Total	100%	100%	100%	100%

Despite the frequency with which the respondents used their local bus service – 20.7 per cent stated every day and 14.2 per cent almost every day – the proportion of the total respondents who used a season ticket or travel pass was smaller (19.2 per cent). The highest proportion of those who did hold a season ticket or travel pass (48.9 per cent) were from Leith. This equated to one quarter of the respondents residing in Leith being in possession of a travel pass, compared to 20.4 per cent in Castlemilk and 9.6 per cent in Coatbridge.

Bus Fares

Thirty-three per cent (n=155) stated that they paid reduced fares. The majority of these fares were paid by people who were aged over 60 (84 per cent) and retired (80.3 per cent). Only 1.3 per cent who were unemployed or seeking work stated that they paid reduced fares. Reduced fares were also found to be not just the preserve of the elderly and retired population but also for those on low incomes: 45.2 per cent of those on gross annual household incomes under £10,300 (that is, weekly income below £199) also paid reduced bus fares.

The average cost of the season ticket/travel pass was found to be £38.12 (standard deviation £71.56) and tended to more often cover either a four week period (29.8 per cent) or a calendar month (15.5 per cent). Twenty-three per cent of respondents stated that their season ticket covered a year. There were some differences in length of time that the travel passes covered for the largest proportions of respondents within each case study areas. A year was the most common period for travel pass holders in Leith (38.1 per cent). In Castlemilk, four weeks was more common, with 39.4 per cent of respondents holding a travel pass which covered that period. In Coatbridge, (77.8 per cent) stated 'other' as the most common response. Since those who specified 'other' were not asked to detail what period this was, it is difficult to establish what period of time that might be, although it is possible to surmise from the information collected during the transport assessment.

All respondents were asked to record how much they spend on bus fares in a typical week. The average spend on bus fares per week for all respondents was £3.79 (standard deviation £5.98). In Leith, the average bus fare was higher than in the other two areas: £4.86 (standard deviation £8.91) compared to £3.59 (standard deviation £3.62) in Castlemilk and £2.73 (standard deviation £2.90) for Coatbridge. Figure 4.1 gives an indication of the distribution of expenditure on bus fares in each case study area.

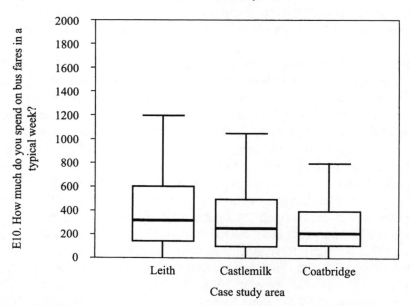

Figure 4.1   Distribution of bus fares in each case study area

Income levels were found to have a significant impact on the amount spent on bus fares. A greater proportion of respondents on lower incomes were also more likely to spend more on bus travel (Table 4.18).

Table 4.18   Bus expenditure per week and household income

Bus expenditure per week	Household income Under £7,700	£7,800–15,500	£15,600 or more	Total
Less than £2–£40	37.6%	40.9%	33.3%	37.4%
Over £2–£40	62.4%	59.1%	66.7%	62.6%
Total	100%	100%	100%	100%

Perception of Local Bus Services and Accessing Timetable Information

Overall most users felt that the service was of a reasonable quality. Buses were on time (55.2 per cent), frequent (63.4), safe (59.1), ticketing arrangements were found to be simple (69.9 per cent). Buses were felt not to perform well in terms of quality of service on the following items: protection against the weather, convenience of changing buses, finding out about routes and services, people on buses are well behaved, cheapness of fares, value for money, facilities at the bus stop and buses are clean. Table 4.19 provides a summary of the results.

When the mean response scores are disaggregated by area (here the lowest mean score indicates a higher level of agreement with the statement in Table 4.20). In Coatbridge, local bus services were perceived to be more frequent and faster, fares were also felt to cheap and offer value for money. In Castlemilk and Coatbridge, finding out about routes and the times of services was felt to be less easy. In Castlemilk, ticketing arrangements were thought to be more simple. All areas perform badly, however, in terms of having services that very randomly reach a mean response value of 3 or above for many items.

The most frequently used methods of accessing bus service timetable information were at the bus stop (24.3 per cent), from the travel centre run by the operator (27.4 per cent), from the bus station (15.9 per cent), or telephone help line (19.2 per cent). Respondents accessed information about the buses (e.g. timetable) least often from the driver (9.1 per cent), from information displayed on the bus (6.0 per cent), from the Internet (0.2 per cent), from friends and relatives (8.5 per cent), library (1.6 per cent) and local shop (1.8 per cent).

Table 4.19 Perception of local bus service

	Agree strongly	Agree	Neither agree nor disagree	Disagree	Disagree strongly
Generally, when you use the bus ...					
the buses are on time	8.5	55.2	17.5	14.5	4.2
the buses are frequent	9.0	63.4	13.4	12	2.2
the buses are fast	5.2	48.3	27.6	16.8	2.2
the buses are comfortable	5.0	54.0	21.9	15.8	3.3
the buses are clean	3.3	44.2	24.3	21.0	7.2
the buses are safe	3.7	59.1	21.7	13.1	2.4
getting on and off buses is easy	7.4	57.3	13.7	15.3	6.3
the ticketing arrangements are simple	11.1	69.9	11.1	5.7	2.2
there is protection against the weather while waiting	1.5	24.1	18.0	39.6	16.8
facilities at bus stops are satisfactory	1.5	28.1	21.7	32.2	16.5
changing buses is convenient	2.8	40.3	32.3	19.0	5.5
changing buses is safe	2.4	55.4	33.4	6.6	2.2
finding out about routes and times of services is easy	5.5	42.5	17.2	25.9	8.9
the kinds of people who travel on buses are well behaved	1.5	46.4	31.1	15.0	6.1
the fares are cheap	3.1	49.9	20.0	20.0	7.0
the fares are good value	4.8	49.5	22.3	16.9	6.4
it takes you directly to destinations you want to go	4.8	58.0	17.3	14.5	5.3

Table 4.20 Perception of local bus services (mean response) in each study area*

Generally, when you use the bus …	Overall	Leith	Castlemilk	Coatbridge
the buses are on time	2.51	2.60	2.71	2.21
the buses are frequent	2.35	2.31	2.59	2.15
the buses are fast	2.63	2.85	2.44	2.57
the buses are comfortable	2.59	2.76	2.48	2.51
the buses are clean	2.85	2.95	3.06	2.52
the buses are safe	2.51	2.34	2.66	2.56
getting on and off buses is easy	2.56	2.65	2.42	2.60
the ticketing arrangements are simple	2.18	2.26	2.08	2.20
there is protection against the weather while waiting	3.46	3.24	3.45	3.70
facilities at bus stops are satisfactory	3.34	3.16	3.41	3.46
changing buses is convenient	2.84	2.98	2.82	2.72
changing buses is safe	2.51	2.50	2.54	2.49
finding out about routes and times of services is easy	2.90	2.60	3.08	3.03
the kinds of people who travel on buses are well behaved	2.78	2.84	2.97	2.53
the fares are cheap	2.78	2.88	2.91	2.53
the fares are good value	2.71	2.74	2.84	2.54
it takes you directly to destinations you want to go	2.58	2.65	2.68	2.39

* This refers to the average response score on a five point scale where agreement strongly with a statement represents 1 and a strong disagreement represents 5. In the table this means tjat those closer to 1 are therefore in a higher level agreement than those closer to 5.

Travel by Local Train

Trains were used infrequently in Coatbridge and Castlemilk:[5] 26.9 per cent of respondents stated that they used them very rarely and 49.2 per cent never. The average rail fare expenditure in a typical week was £2.24 (standard deviation £7.42). Nonetheless, of those using trains 31.3 per cent stated that they used reduced rail fares. Many of those eligible for reduced rail fares were predominantly aged over 60 (73.8 per cent). However, there was also a significant proportion who were under pensionable age (26.8 per cent), and these were found to be in receipt of disability and incapacity benefits. Only 13.4 per cent stated they used a rail season ticket and a considerable proportion (35.7 per cent) of those stated that it was a zone card which allowed them travel on buses, trains and the underground.

Restrictions in Use of Public Transport

Travel by public transport was restricted by a number of reasons. Most people stated that they had concerns about their safety after dark, and of these 56.4 per cent were female. Concerns for personal safety on public transport during the day was found to be a major issue for those on lower incomes, especially under £150 per week (59.4 per cent). The other factors are listed below:

- 7.4 per cent because of concerns about personal safety during the day;
- 44.4 per cent because of concerns about personal safety after dark;
- 18.5 per cent due to the cost of fares;
- 32.4 per cent due to lack of information about public transport;
- 16.9 per cent felt they were unable to board vehicles easily or safely;
- 21.4 per cent felt they had difficulty in travelling with prams or buggies;
- 29.4 per cent due to the times of services;
- 30.2 per cent due to the routes served;
- 17.5 per cent because of the lack of facilities for children;
- 25.5 per cent due to the reliability of services.

Restrictions on public transport travel was found to differ little in terms of car availability. None of these concerns were found to be statistically significantly at the 95 per cent level (Table 4.20).

Table 4.20   Restrictions on public transport travel and car access, %
of respondents stating yes

	Regular car access	No access
Concerns about personal safety during the day	7.0	11.1
Concerns about personal safety after dark	41.1	43.4
The cost of fares	20.7	14.5
Lack of information about public transport	39.4	27.3
Being unable to board vehicles easily and safely	12.9	27.3
Difficulty in travelling with prams and buggies	25.7	18.8
The times of services	29.1	32.7
The routes served	35.9	27.8
The lack of facilities for children	21.6	20.4
Reliability of services	29.6	29.1

Travel by Taxi

Frequency of Use

Taxis are the ultimate form of demand responsive transport, but in the case study areas seemed to be rarely used (8 per cent never and 27 per cent very rarely). Nonetheless 37 per cent stated they used taxis between one and three times per week. There were, however, some marked differences in taxi usage between the case study areas. Of the respondents who used taxis every day, the overwhelming majority (72.2 per cent) were from Coatbridge. This was also the case for those using taxis almost every day, where 63.6 per cent of respondents resided in Coatbridge. In general, taxi usage was higher for those living in Castlemilk and Coatbridge compared to Leith (Table 4.21). Frequent users of public transport are also young, aged 16–30.

Taxis are seldom used in these communities as they are regarded as being expensive forms of transport and because it was felt that there were good public transport options available elsewhere. Conversely, the main reasons why respondents did use taxis because it offered a fast (16.3 per cent), convenient (38.4 per cent) service that was direct (17 per cent). People also used taxis to avoid drink driving (18.5 per cent), if there was no other public transport alternative available (22.3 per cent) and if they had a heavy shopping load to carry (12.9 per cent).

Table 4.21   Frequency of taxi use, by case study area

	Leith %	Castlemilk %	Coatbridge %	Overall %
		Case study areas		
Every day	0.5	2.2	7.2	3.3
Almost every day	2.1	2.2	7.7	4.0
2–3 times per week	18.0	19.7	17.7	18.4
Once per week	16.4	18.0	21.5	18.6
Once a fortnight	11.1	7.9	6.6	8.6
Once a month	15.3	15.2	5.5	12.0
Very rarely	31.2	28.1	21.5	27.0
Never	5.3	6.7	12.2	8.0

Taxi cards, which entitle the user to reduced taxi fares, were used by 5 per cent of respondents. The majority of these were from Leith (53.6 per cent) compared to 17.9 per cent in Castlemilk and 28.6 per cent in Coatbridge. These users were concentrated in the 30–40 age band (28.5 per cent) and in the over 70 age band (32.1 per cent).

Community Transport

Community transport is always envisaged by policy makers as an option to mainstream public transport. In some circumstances community transport organisations can provide services that can plug the gap in terms of accessing scheduled services. Nonetheless, there is a large access issue for this form of transport. The majority (61.7 per cent) of respondents in this study were aware of community transport schemes (such as dial-a-ride, shopping buses and social work buses) operating in their area, but of these only 4.8 per cent (n=11) stated that they had used a community transport scheme. The highest proportion (33.8 per cent) of those who were aware of community transport schemes were permanently retired from work and could only walk less than 100 yards unaided. A higher proportion of respondents in Coatbridge (86.2 per cent) and Castlemilk (57.1 per cent) were aware of such schemes than in Leith (26.1 per cent). Usage was highest in Coatbridge. The main purpose of their use of community transport was for shopping. None of the respondents used community transport to travel to work or education.

Walking and Cycling

Frequency of Trips

In these three communities walking is a significant mode of transport. Most people walked every day (60.8 per cent), whereas the majority of respondents never made journeys by bicycle (79 per cent). Only a small proportion stated they never walked (4.4 per cent) (Table 4.22). These were predominantly women and those unable to walk less a 100 yards unaided. In Coatbridge and Castlemilk people tended to walk less than in Leith. 73 per cent of those residing in Leith walked every day compared to 59 per cent in Castlemilk and 49 per cent in Coatbridge.

Table 4.22   Trip frequency, walking and cycling

Frequency	Walking n=551	Cycling n=538
Every day	60.8	2.6
Almost every day	10.0	2.0
2–3 times per week	13.6	3.0
Once per week	4.5	3.3
Once per 2 weeks	0.4	0.4
Once per month	0.5	2.0
Very rarely	5.8	7.6
Never	4.4	79.0

Levels of car access have little or no impact on the level of walking (Table 4.23). In comparison with this finding car access seems to have impact on the levels of cycling (Table 4.24). Having no access at all to a car does account for higher levels of cycle use.

For those who did walk to their destination, the main reasons they said they walked are because they enjoy it (31.3 per cent), because the journeys are short distances (44.4 per cent) and to keep fit and healthy (39.3 per cent). This was similar to the main reasons given by cyclists, whose main reason for choosing to cycle was because they liked it (8.2 per cent) or to keep fit and healthy (9.2 per cent).

Table 4.23   Car access and frequency of journeys involving walking

Frequency of journeys involving walking	Car access			Total
	Regular car access	*Relying on lifts*	*No access at all*	
Every day	56%	62.8%	64.3%	60.3%
Almost every day	9.1%	10%	10.7%	9.7%
2 or 3 times a week	16.3%	12.6%	10.7%	13.9%
Once a week	7.2%	3.7%	–	4.7%
Once a fortnight	1%	–	–	0.4%
Once a month	–	0.7%	1.8%	0.6%
Very rarely	6.2%	5.9%	5.4%	6.0%
Never	4.3%	4.1%	7.1%	4.5%
	100%	100%	100%	100%

Table 4.24   Car access and frequency of journeys involving cycling

Frequency of journeys involving cycling	Car access			Total
	Regular car access	*Relying on lifts*	*No access at all*	
Every day	2.4%	1.5%	7.3%	2.5%
Almost every day	3.4%	1.1%	–	1.9%
2 or 3 times a week	3.9%	2.3%	1.8%	2.9%
Once a week	4.9%	2.7%	1.8%	3.5%
Once a fortnight	1%	–	–	0.4%
Once a month	3.9%	1.1%	–	2.1%
Very rarely	11.2%	4.6%	9.1%	7.7%
Never	69.3%	86.6%	80%	79.1%
	100%	100%	100%	100%

Conclusions

Data from the survey of households in Leith, Castlemilk and Coatbridge indicate that transport plays an important role in helping to shape experiences, by residents in these areas, of social exclusion. Physical barriers have been found to impact to a higher degree on the elderly and people with health problems. Significant difficulties were experienced where travel involved walking and standing for at least 10 minutes. Reported difficulties were also found when using taxis and boarding buses. Disabled people, especially those with chest/breathing difficulties and a disability connected with the arms and legs, also experienced physical exclusion.

The study found that women are less likely to have held a driving licence, both full and provisional, and are as a result more likely to use local bus services and rely on lifts. Reliance on lifts in a car is also a feature of travel for those with health problems and this may be a more workable solution for meeting individual mobility needs where local support networks are in place, i.e. in circumstances where it is relatively easier to obtain lifts in the car from friends and family. Men were more likely to have regular car access, whereas women are more likely to have no access at all to a car.

Tenure has a significant impact on access to a car. Respondents who pay rent in the public and private housing sector are less likely to have access to a car at all. It may, therefore, also be the case that lack of access to a car and lower income can geographically restrict housing choices. A significant proportion of respondents in the survey, in each study area, stated that they would like to move to improve their housing circumstances, but also because of a combination of noise, neighbours and the poor environment.

For those in employment, a small proportion of respondents had stated that transport considerations had prevented them from accepting a job offer. This was also the case for those seeking work and in full-time education. In Leith and Castlemilk, a greater proportion of respondents stated that they would move to improve transport links and accessibility.

Economic exclusion refers to the high monetary or temporal costs of travel that can prevent or limit access to facilities or jobs and thus income. Car use is strongly associated with higher income levels, whereas lower income groups are more reliant on public transport and on lifts. Public transport use and reliance on lifts were generally found to result in longer journey times. A greater proportion of those on lower incomes pay over £2.40 for bus fares than those on higher incomes. This means that, relative to other income groups, people in lower income groups can pay more for their public transport in terms of their income and also have larger travel times when accessing the same range of goods and services by those in higher income groups. Fuel expenditure on cars is, as would be expected, higher amongst higher income groups.

Single parent families and single person households were found to account for a significant proportion of those within lower income groups. It is these groups that are likely to feel the adverse consequences of reliance on public transport the most. In this survey, nearly one quarter of respondents stated that they were worried about money almost all the time. There was little evidence of those on lower incomes paying reduced fares or making use of season tickets.

The perception of bus service frequency corresponds with the view that reliance on public transport makes it more difficult to access particular facilities, especially during week day evenings and on Sundays. Access to bus stops was high with a significant proportion in each case study area stating that the bus stop that was used most often was within a six minute walk (over 80 per cent in each case study area). Access to the bus stop is, however, problematic for the elderly and those with a disability. Taxis were not widely used by the elderly but tended to be used more frequently by those on higher incomes and in younger age groups.

Fear-based exclusion refers to circumstances where worry, fear and even terror influence how public spaces and public transport are used, and space exclusion refers to situations where security and space management strategies can discourage socially excluded individuals from using public transport spaces. Analysis has revealed a significant link between disability and concerns about personal safety after dark There was also limited evidence from the survey that concerns about personal safety and the quality of the local neighbourhood were contributory factors in reasons why respondents wanted to move from the area. There was little other evidence from this survey to suggest that the way public space and public transport services are managed contributes to fear and space exclusion. This does not necessarily mean that these are not important aspects of social exclusion in these case study areas, but may be indicative of avoidance strategies and coping behaviour.

Notes

1   These results can be compared to those of the Scottish Household Survey where 63.4 per cent currently hold a full driving licence (car or motorcycle), 6 per cent currently hold a provisional licence, 0.2 per cent are currently disqualified from driving, 0.9 per cent have their licence suspended on medical grounds and 29.5 per cent have never held a UK driving licence.

2   The Scottish Household Survey found that 69.7 per cent drove every day, 11.4 per cent drove at least three times a week, 6.8 per cent drove once or twice a week, 1.7 per cent drove at least two or three times a week, 0.8 per cent drove at least once a month, 2.7 per cent drove less than once a month, and 6.8 per cent drove never.

3   These figures are not directly comparable to the Scottish Household Survey, which asked a random sample of respondents in Scotland whether there were any motor vehicles normally available for use by members of the household: 63.6 per cent answered 'yes'. This proportion

drops to 36 per cent among very low income households and 52 per cent in disadvantaged council estates. The numbers of motor vehicles available for use were recorded in the survey and are as follows: one – 67.8 per cent; two – 27 per cent; three – 4.2 per cent; four – 0.7 per cent. The quota sampling methods used in this study suppressed the number of car users. Further information on the study methodology is available in an annex of this report.

4   The Scottish Household Survey found that 54.4 per cent of respondents lived within three minutes or less walk of their nearest bus stop. Thirty per cent with 4–6 minutes, 9.8 per cent within 7–13 minutes walk, 4.6 per cent had a walk of over 14 minutes to their nearest bus stop.

5   In Leith there is no direct access to local rail services. Questions on rail were only asked in Coatbridge and Castlemilk.

Chapter 5

Access to Local Services
and Journey Time

Introduction

Variations in car access whether through regular car access, relying on lifts to
no access at all has a profound impact on quality of life. It determines how
frequently goods and services can be accessed, and if services and activities
located outside the local neighbourhood can be travelled to within a reasonable
time. In Chapter 4 we have seen that transport disadvantage and as a
consequence transport-related social exclusion is unevenly distributed in as
far as its' impact is experienced by certain groups. Women are less likely to
hold full and provisional driving licences and are as a result more likely to
use bus services and rely on lifts. Lower levels of car access can also be found
amongst the elderly and disabled. Walking and public transport play a key
role in these communities for both men, women and all income groups.

This chapter provides a detailed account of the mode choice to access
local services and the role of time, in terms of journey time – that is the time
spent travelling to access these facilities. The data analysed in this chapter
provide a record of the mode of transport used most frequently, the travel time
and the classification of key destinations by their location. These destinations
included the local shop, post office, bank, supermarket and a range of others.
The data also provides an indication of the frequency with which activities
are undertaken (for example grocery shopping trips, evenings out for leisure
purposes, attending educational classes) and the mode they used.

Access to Local Services

In these communities walking is the dominant mode of transport to most types
of activity in each area that is with the exception of trips to the cinema, bus
station, hospital, and supermarket. For trips to the supermarket, bank, doctor,
dentist, cinema, and to the hospital access to a car is important but less so
than the bus. Many of these activities lie outwith the local neighbourhood.

Travel by bicycle, motorbike, community transport and train accounts for very small proportions of the modal split for each journey and activity type and as it is less than 1 per cent in all cases these modes have been excluded from the table below. Table 5.1 provides a summary of the percentage of respondents using each mode to access a variety of destinations. It shows the predominance of walking for many of the journeys. The lower levels of car dependence exhibited in this table conform with patterns of car access discussed in Chapter 4.

Table 5.1   Percentage of respondents using mode to access facilities

	% of respondents					
	Car (driver)	Car (passenger)	Taxi	Bus	Walk	Never use
Local shop	9.6	2.5	1.1	9.3	74.0	1.8
Post office	9.4	2.2	.7	6.0	77.3	3.4
Supermarket	22.0	9.4	2.9	25.2	36.3	2.0
Bank	16.8	5.3	2.2	27.5	38.4	7.5
Doctor	16.7	6.2	5.4	24.5	42.1	2.7
Chemist	11.3	4.2	.9	12.0	66.9	2.9
Dentist	16.6	4.4	2.4	20.9	39.7	13.8
Sports/leisure centre	14.3	3.1	.7	13.7	26.0	41.0
Cinema	16.1	9.2	4.2	27.9	8.3	33.2
Pub	2.4	1.6	7.5	13.2	32.2	42.2
Railway station	6.0	3.3	5.3	29.7	24.7	28.9
Bus station	4.0	2.6	4.2	41.2	9.3	36.7
Primary school	3.3	.9	.5	1.3	28.0	65.6
Secondary school	3.8	.9	.4	3.1	19.7	71.8
Library	9.7	2.9	.9	11.3	46.4	27.0
Church	6.4	4.6	.9	4.7	41.2	41.3
Hospital	21.7	10.6	8.9	42.8	2.9	9.5
Local government office	7.7	2.6	.5	20.8	14.2	53.1

Walking dominates as the mode used to access most facilities, and because of this dominance there is little or no variation in this pattern by gender, income or by case study area. However, gender, income and levels of car access do impact on the journey times of people accessing these services. There are some differences in, for example, journeys to the cinema where the most frequent mode chosen by women is the bus whereas men choose 'never use' most frequently. Conversely, men choose 'walk' to the pub most often whereas women choose 'never use'. For each case study area, the most frequent mode for most destinations is walking. Sports/leisure centre and cinema are the exceptions to this. For sports leisure centre 'never use' is chosen more frequently in Leith and Coatbridge and for cinema 'bus' is chosen more frequently in Leith and Castlemilk, whereas 'never use' is the most frequent response by residents of Coatbridge. In comparison with the other areas in this study, car use plays a greater role in Coatbridge. This is a reflection of the relatively poor bus services in the area (Table 5.2).

Table 5.2   Percentage of respondents using mode to access facilities, Coatbridge

	% of respondents					
	Car (driver)	Car (passenger)	Taxi	Bus	Walk	Never use
Local shop	16.5	4.9	1.6	13.2	62.6	0.5
Post office	16.4	3.3	1.1	4.4	71.0	3.8
Supermarket	26.8	10.9	7.7	38.8	12.6	2.2
Bank	24.6	10.9	6.0	38.8	12.0	7.1
Doctor	27.3	11.5	9.3	38.8	8.7	3.3
Chemist	22.4	8.2	1.6	20.2	41.5	4.4
Dentist	24.6	8.2	3.8	27.9	23.0	11.5
Sports/leisure centre	17.7	6.6	1.7	14.9	17.7	41.4
Cinema	17.7	14.9	7.2	7.2	21.5	30.4
Pub	1.6	2.2	11.5	3.3	34.4	46.4
Railway station	8.2	4.4	3.8	7.1	49.7	25.7
Bus station	4.9	1.6	1.1	24.0	12.0	54.1
Primary school	3.8	1.6	0.5	1.1	35.2	57.1
Secondary school	6.0	1.6	0.5	2.7	24.7	63.7
Library	15.9	6.6	1.1	11.0	40.1	24.7
Church	11.5	6.0	2.2	2.7	56.0	20.9
Hospital	28.6	17.0	12.1	31.9	2.2	5.5
Local government office	12.1	6.0	1.1	25.8	13.2	41.2

Activity Locations

The location of each of the key destinations that were used by residents, whether in the local neighbourhood, city centre, another suburb, or another town, has an important impact on mode choice. Many facilities were found to be located within the local neighbourhood, thereby accounting for the significance of walking to these locations (as discussed in Table 5.1). The Table 5.3 below provides a summary of the location of the key destinations used by residents in each of the case study areas. It shows a predominance of many of the key destinations to be located within, what respondents classified as, the local neighbourhood. In the local neighbourhood walking dominated the travel patterns within Leith and Castlemilk. In Coatbridge, compared to Leith and Castlemilk, the analysis showed a greater tendency of the respondents to use car and bus for local neighbourhood journeys. Also in Coatbridge, respondents more frequently accessed goods and services in the city centre by these modes of transport (Table 5.4).

Table 5.3   Percentage of respondents stating location of facilities

	% of respondents stating location within …			
	Local neighbourhood	*City centre*	*Another suburb*	*Another town*
Local shop	95.9	3.0	1.1	0.0
Post office	94.2	3.0	2.4	0.4
Supermarket	67.8	13.7	17.6	0.9
Bank	65.6	22.3	11.7	0.4
Doctor	69.1	15.6	14.3	0.9
Chemist	87.6	9.0	3.0	0.4
Dentist	67.1	12.6	17.1	3.2
Sports/leisure centre	70.3	10.3	17.0	2.4
Cinema	22.7	41.1	33.4	2.7
Pub	61.7	24.0	12.8	1.6
Railway station	38.2	54.0	6.7	1.0
Bus station	16.4	76.4	3.2	4.0
Primary school	94.7	1.6	3.7	0.0
Secondary school	88.3	1.3	9.7	0.6
Library	82.3	10.4	6.3	1.0
Church	91.0	4.7	4.4	0.0
Hospital	14.0	17.4	53.2	15.4
Local government office	51.0	39.5	8.0	1.5

Table 5.4   Percentage of respondents stating location of facilities, Coatbridge

	% of respondents stating location within …			
	Local neighbourhood	*City centre*	*Another suburb*	*Another town*
Local shop	93.3	6.7	0.0	0.0
Post office	94.8	4.0	0.6	0.6
Supermarket	59.3	36.7	2.3	1.7
Bank	60.1	34.5	4.2	1.2
Doctor	54.6	40.8	3.4	1.1
Chemist	75.1	20.2	4.0	0.6
Dentist	62.4	25.5	7.0	5.1
Sports/leisure centre	66.7	23.1	5.6	4.6
Cinema	64.2	9.8	23.6	2.4
Pub	82.5	12.4	2.1	3.1
Railway station	77.9	14.5	5.3	2.3
Bus station	38.1	39.3	8.3	14.3
Primary school	94.7	0.0	5.3	0.0
Secondary school	92.1	1.6	4.8	1.6
Library	77.8	14.1	5.9	2.2
Church	96.4	1.4	2.2	0.0
Hospital	21.9	4.7	31.4	42.0
Local government office	60.7	34.6	1.9	2.8

For trips to local shops, schools, the post office and library a significantly large proportion of trips are made on foot in each case study area. This is reflected in the high proportion of trips made within the local neighbourhood for these activities and the low journey times. A significant proportion of journeys were found to last under 10 minutes. Trips to the bank, sports and leisure facilities, the supermarket, doctor, dentist and chemist in Leith and Castlemilk were found to be largely undertaken on foot, although a growing proportion of trips in these areas are made by bus and car to access these services. Coatbridge is significantly different to Leith and Castlemilk in that car use is higher for each of these activities. The higher car use levels are not only associated with trips to access the services outside the local neighbourhood but also within it. For access to the cinema and hospitals, some stark contrasts were found between the three areas. In Leith and Castlemilk access to cinema facilities is more reliant on bus use, whereas in Coatbridge the car is the more important mode. This is due to a larger proportion of trips being made outwith the neighbourhood to the city centre and another suburb or town. For access to hospital facilities the main form of transport is the bus and car. Analysis of the data by level of car access clearly indicates that travel times taken to access services are generally higher where there is no access and where residents rely on lifts from a friend of someone in their household.

Journey Times

Journey time is clearly strongly inter-related with mode choice and activity location. The discussion here is taken further in terms of the distribution of these times by gender, income group and level of access to a car. Table 5.5 provides an indication of the average journey times taken to access these facilities in minutes.

Table 5.5   Average time (minutes) taken to access facilities, case study areas

| | Average time taken (minutes) | | | |
	Overall	*Leith*	*Castlemilk*	*Coatbridge*
Local shop	6.6	6.2	6.5	6.8
Post office	6.6	5.7	7.1	7.1
Supermarket	10.5	10.6	9.7	11.2
Bank	11.7	8.8	13.1	13.2
Doctor	10.8	10.6	10.4	11.5
Chemist	7.7	6.6	7.5	9.2
Dentist	11.9	14.1	10.2	11.5
Sports/leisure centre	10.9	11.6	10.4	10.7
Cinema	20.0	23.1	24.5	12.7
Pub	12.5	13.4	15.6	8.5
Railway station	14.8	17.0	17.9	10.0
Bus station	19.3	17.0	25.5	15.1
Primary school	7.6	10.5	7.3	6.3
Secondary school	10.5	11.3	11.1	9.5
Library	9.4	9.7	9.2	9.2
Church	8.3	10.1	8.7	7.2
Hospital	21.4	25.1	20.7	18.7
Local government office	15.0	15.3	18.6	11.8

Identifying the average time taken to access different facilities in each case study area shows that the majority of the facilities are within a reasonable distance (in terms of time). The diagram below illustrates the time taken to reach each facility where the mean is illustrated alongside the standard deviation and the range of responses made. From this diagram (Figure 5.1) it is possible to see where responses differ the most, for example, in the time taken to reach the hospital, cinema and bus station.

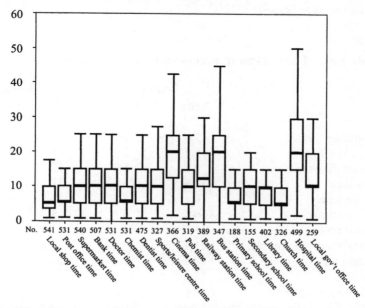

Figure 5.1   Distribution of times taken to access facilities

Note: all outliers and extremes have been excluded from this figure.

The average time taken to visit basic services varies when examined by gender. Women take longer to access most facilities, with the exception of trips to the sports/leisure centre, church and primary school, where their travel times are lower. However, for all other key destinations men are able to access these facilities more quickly due to their higher levels of car use (Table 5.6). For example, the average time taken to visit the local shop by car is 7.1 minutes for men and 5.7 minutes for women. By bus, it takes men on average 11.4 minutes and women 10.2 minutes. When walking, men reach the local shop a little quicker (4.8 minutes) than women, who take 6.7 minutes on average. The differences in the average time taken to reach the local shop according to employment status does reveal some differences although these are small. Those who classed themselves as 'sick or disabled' took longer to travel by bus (15 minutes) to the local shop than the other groups, who took 10 minutes on average. This was not always the case for other destinations – no clear pattern emerges. However, the pattern remains that those who take the shortest time to reach, for example, the local shop are those who walk, which might account for the reason that 'walk' is the most frequent mode used for most of the facilities accessed.

Table 5.6   Time taken to access facilities by gender

	Men		Women	
	Mean	*Std deviation*	*Mean*	*Std deviation*
Local shop time	5.6	4.1	7.1	5.1
Post office time	5.4	3.9	7.4	5.8
Supermarket time	9.1	5.6	11.3	7.4
Bank time	11.6	26.6	11.7	9.4
Doctor time	10.1	8.3	11.1	8.3
Chemist time	6.8	6.1	8.3	6.0
Dentist time	11.6	14.7	11.9	9.1
Sports/leisure centre time	11.1	7.8	10.8	7.9
Cinema time	18.2	10.5	20.9	10.9
Pub time	12.6	19.1	12.4	9.5
Railway station time	14.9	14.6	14.8	8.5
Bus station time	17.4	10.4	20.4	11.2
Primary school time	9.0	7.8	7.0	4.8
Secondary school time	9.9	6.4	10.9	7.7
Library time	9.3	6.7	9.5	6.7
Church time	8.6	6.6	8.2	6.0
Hospital time	21.7	17.9	21.2	10.7
Local government office time	14.6	10.1	15.3	9.9

In general, the average time taken to travel to local facilities was longest for those travelling by bus, or car, and shortest for those walking.

The time taken to reach local facilities was also examined in relation to car access, where it was observed that it was, not surprisingly, quicker for people to access services if they have regular access to a car: if they have occasional access to a car then their mean travel time increases. Interestingly though, those with no car access give a similar travel time as those with a car.

Table 5.7　Time taken (minutes) to access facilities by level of car access

Car access	Regular car access		Relying on lifts		No car access	
	Mean	Std deviation	Mean	Std deviation	Mean	Std deviation
Local shop time	5.5	4.5	7.3	4.9	7.2	4.8
Post office time	5.4	4.4	7.6	5.5	6.7	5.4
Supermarket time	9.4	6.1	11.4	7.5	10.9	6.0
Bank time	12.1	26.7	11.8	8.3	9.9	6.6
Doctor time	10.0	9.0	11.6	8.5	10.7	5.9
Chemist time	6.5	4.8	8.7	6.8	8.1	5.9
Dentist time	12.0	14.6	12.1	9.5	10.7	5.9
Sports/leisure centre time	10.4	7.0	11.1	8.2	11.7	9.0
Cinema time	17.7	9.3	21.9	12.2	20.6	9.1
Pub time	11.6	10.7	12.7	10.2	10.6	8.5
Railway station time	13.1	8.0	15.8	13.3	16.8	10.5
Bus station time	17.5	8.9	19.9	11.9	20.4	12.1
Primary school time	7.0	5.6	8.2	6.7	7.0	3.6
Secondary school time	9.3	5.5	12.0	8.8	8.6	4.8
Library time	9.1	6.7	9.5	6.9	9.9	5.9
Church time	7.5	6.0	8.8	6.3	9.1	6.3
Hospital time	17.7	10.2	22.8	11.8	29.8	27.4
Local government office time	14.3	9.5	15.4	10.1	15.4	12.2

Also those without car access give a less varied range of travel times – possibly as they use only their local facilities and can accurately estimate how long it takes to get there. Those who travel by car regularly have a much broader spatial area to which they have access and consequently have a broader range of times to get there (Table 5.7). Income levels also impact on journey times considerably. Those residents on salaries over £15,500 had lower mean journey times for accessing facilities compared to lower income groups (Table 5.8). Journey times are much greater for those reliant on lifts from others and who have no access to a car.

Frequency of Trips

Residents in each of the case study areas recorded the number of times they had undertaken a range of activities in the previous week, in addition to stating the main mode that they used to access these activities. A summary of the frequency with which these activities were undertaken is provided in Table 5.9.

These activities were explored in relation to the mode used, which was also recorded in this question. The analysis demonstrated a clear difference, with those on a lower income using more variety of transport modes while those on higher incomes tend to use their cars. This confirms the evidence discussed in Chapter 4. Analysis of the relationship shows that those on a lower income are far more likely to do their grocery shopping trips on foot than those on a higher income, who are more likely to go to the shops by car. Those on low incomes are also less likely to use out-of-town retail parks whereas those on a higher income are more likely to drive to them by car. Those on low incomes are more likely to visit their friends and relatives on foot, whereas those on higher incomes are more likely to drive there. The mode used may also have a relationship with the frequency with which people have undertaken the activities listed. In the first column of Table 5.7, under 'none', particularly high proportions of the entire sample are evident. Town centre shopping trips and shopping trips to out-of-town retail stores were notable, although not the highest in terms of non-use, at 44.3 per cent and 78.1 per cent. Evenings out for leisure purposes (54.2 per cent) and days out for leisure purposes (67.3 per cent) were also particularly high.

The frequency of the activities undertaken appeared to be related to car access in a way that might be expected. For grocery trips, all modes play an important role – public transport and walking are as important as the car.

Table 5.8   Time taken (minutes) to access facilities by income group

Income group	Under £7,700		£7,800–£15,500		Over £15,500	
	Mean	Std deviation	Mean	Std deviation	Mean	Std deviation
Local shop time	7.2	5.0	5.9	4.5	5.8	4.4
Post office time	7.6	5.5	5.7	4.0	5.5	4.1
Supermarket time	11.2	7.6	10.5	7.1	9.9	5.6
Bank time	11.3	8.1	12.9	30.2	10.9	10.3
Doctor time	11.7	8.6	11.3	9.2	9.5	7.8
Chemist time	8.5	7.4	7.7	5.7	6.6	4.6
Dentist time	11.4	8.2	11.1	9.3	13.6	16.7
Sports/leisure centre time	10.7	7.8	11.9	8.9	10.8	7.9
Cinema time	22.0	13.2	19.5	9.2	18.6	9.4
Pub time	14.0	23.9	12.8	11.3	11.0	8.6
Railway station time	14.7	9.0	16.2	16.3	14.0	8.3
Bus station time	19.4	12.3	20.5	11.3	17.7	8.2
Primary school time	7.8	5.6	7.7	5.8	7.6	6.9
Secondary school time	10.2	7.7	11.7	8.3	9.3	5.7
Library time	10.2	7.3	9.6	7.2	8.4	5.5
Church time	8.4	6.1	8.2	6.8	7.8	5.8
Hospital time	25.4	14.1	21.5	17.0	18.3	10.3
Local government office time	15.5	9.9	14.8	9.6	13.1	8.4

Table 5.9   Frequency of activities undertaken

| | % of respondents undertaking activity | | | |
	None	*Once*	*2 to 3 times*	*4 or more times*
Grocery shopping trips	9.3	29.9	35.4	25.4
Town centre shopping trips	44.3	33.2	18.2	4.4
Retail park shopping trips	78.1	17.6	3.8	0.5
Collecting prescriptions	64.5	30.3	4.4	0.7
Visiting friends/relatives	35.8	24.4	25.1	14.7
Evenings out for leisure purposes	54.2	23.7	17.8	4.2
Taking children to and from school	80.8	2.3	3.4	13.6
Taking children to other activities	81.7	7.5	7.0	3.8
Days out for leisure purposes	67.3	20.4	10.8	1.5
Voluntary work/duties	89.8	5.6	3.9	0.7
Attended adult education	88.7	5.6	2.0	3.7

Indeed, for town centre trips walking, bus and car passenger classifications had larger proportions making more than one journey per week, whereas the use of the bus to collect prescriptions is important in comparison to other modes. For frequent travel to the retail park having access to a car is important, but walking plays a significant role for 2–3 journeys per week (50 per cent). For higher frequency journeys to visit friends and relatives a larger proportion journeys are on foot and by bus. For infrequent trips these are more likely to be made by car.

The differences in gender are less marked. In visiting friends and relatives the proportions within each category of frequency were approximately equal. This is similar for those who had evenings out for leisure purposes – although a slightly higher proportion (57.7 per cent) of women had no evenings out in the last week compared to 48.3 per cent of men – and for those who had days out for leisure purposes. In the other trips made which are less leisure-based – for example, taking children to school/college, voluntary work/duties, attending adult education – the gender proportions are again similar.

In general, the relationships between activities and income were not statistically significant. This was only the case for days out for leisure purposes, evenings out for leisure purposes and grocery shopping trips where, for example, those on a lower income were less likely to go out for the evening while those on higher income are more likely to go out. For those residents making grocery shopping trips in the past week and earning under £7,700, the

Table 5.10 Mode and trip frequency

Trip type	Trip frequency per week	Car driver %	Car passenger %	Bus %	Walk %
Grocery	0	4.3	8.9	2.6	3.0
	1	41.4	50.0	34.8	15.0
	2–3	41.4	33.9	39.1	37.5
	4+	12.9	7.1	23.5	44.5
Town centre	0	22.5	24.1	24.9	23.3
	1	47.9	27.6	46.1	36.7
	2–3	26.8	37.9	22.0	40.0
	4+	2.8	10.3	7.1	0.0
Retail park	0	37.3	55.1	58.0	33.3
	1	48.2	37.7	40.0	16.7
	2–3	13.3	5.8	2.0	50.0
	4+	1.2	1.4	0.0	0.0
Collecting prescriptions	0	44.7	35.7	27.1	33.3
	1	47.4	42.9	62.5	16.7
	2–3	5.3	14.3	10.4	50.0
	4+	2.6	7.1	0.0	0.0
Visiting friends and relatives	0	16.7	26.5	20.4	8.8
	1	34.4	44.9	32.3	22.6
	2–3	27.1	18.4	35.5	41.6
	4+	21.9	10.2	11.8	27.0
Evenings out – leisure	0	30.8	31.9	25.6	16.9
	1	36.5	44.7	31.7	37.7
	2–3	30.8	19.1	30.5	35.1
	4+	1.9	4.3	12.2	10.4

highest proportion (34.2 per cent) made grocery shopping trips 'four or more times' in the past week, whereas for those earning £7,800–£15,500 and for those earning £15,600 or more the highest proportions made trips two to three times a week. For town centre shopping trips the proportions making each number of trips was similar for all household income categories. The proportions were similar for each income category in the number of times that respondents visited friends and relatives – the most noticeable difference was in the higher proportions of those earning under £7,700 in making no visits and in making 'four or more visits'.

Conclusions

Poor transport provision and resulting inaccessibility can create patterns of exclusion. Geographical exclusion may be felt to a greater degree by residents in localities on the edge of a city/town or a free-standing town where access to a car is nonexistent or where a reliance is based on lifts. In Coatbridge, a free-standing town where bus services are relatively poor compared to the other two case study areas, there is a greater reliance on the car even for making trips within the neighbourhood. Evidence also indicates a greater diversity of activity patterns and mode choice in this area.

Exclusion from facilities can occur where the distance of facilities from people's homes can make access difficult, especially for those without a car. Evidence indicates that low income groups and women are more likely to suffer from this dimension of exclusion where access to facilities is made easier by car use. For trips within the neighbourhood, evidence from the survey indicates that walking is a dominant mode of transport, although there are circumstances where travel by car accounts for a higher share of trips even within the neighbourhood. Car use rises for trips to out-of-town retail facilities, hospital, bank and doctor. There are, however, high levels of public transport use for these activities as well, but travel times are lower for those who can access a car.

Respondents without a car tended to go less frequently to retail shopping park facilities and on trips to visit friends. Differences by gender are less marked on these trips. Lower income groups are, however, more likely to make regular grocery trips, whereas those on higher incomes made fewer trips per week.

The analysis demonstrates a strong link between local neighbourhood and the pattern of mode choice in each case study area. Respondents chose 'local neighbourhood' as the most frequent response for the location of key facilities that they accessed. Journey time was inter-related with mode choice and location. In the local neighbourhood, walking dominated travel patterns within Leith and Castlemilk. In Coatbridge, compared to Leith and Castlemilk, the analysis showed a greater tendency of the respondents to use car and bus for local neighbourhood journeys. Also in Coatbridge, respondents accessed goods and services in the city centre by these modes. This fits with the findings regarding car use and ownership, discussed earlier in Chapter 4, where the highest proportion of licence holders driving every day resided within Coatbridge. Coatbridge also had the highest proportion of car ownership compared with the other two case study areas. Castlemilk had the highest proportion of respondents who never drive, and Leith had the highest proportion of licence holders but the lowest proportion of respondents who drive regularly.

Evidence on time taken to access facilities, especially for those journeys outwith the neighbourhood and to facilities in relatively remote locations such as hospitals and out of town shopping facilities, indicated that time spent travelling is higher especially for those trips made by bus. It is therefore clear that bus users – who are more likely to be people on lower incomes, women, the disabled and the elderly – are spending longer to access particular goods and services, especially those outside their local neighbourhood.

Access to a car makes journey times lower but at the same time gives more flexibility in terms of the choice of location at which to access particular goods and services.

Chapter 6

Local Authority Response
and the Public Transport Network

Introduction

Transport disadvantage or deprivation can induce or exacerbate conditions that can lead to the exclusion of individuals and communities. The availability of a car, adequate household income and gender are key determinants of transport disadvantage if measured by differences in journey time to key destinations, for example. It would be fair to say at this point in time that there is a growing awareness of transport and social exclusion (Hine and Mitchell, 2001). Sinclair et al. (2001) have also noted that local authorities tend to be more familiar with standard transport issues.

This chapter provides experiential evidence of local authorities and operators in providing public transport in the three case study areas. The identification of solutions to the link between transport and social exclusion also reflects a wider problem that in the current operational environment it is very difficult to target resources geographically or at particular groups and potentially even more difficult to justify the targeting of those resources at the expense of other areas and groups whose experiences of the transport system may be similar.

City Centre – Leith, City of Edinburgh

Views of the Network

In the Leith area both operators and the local authority viewed the density of the bus network as being of a high standard compared to other areas in the city. However, they recognised that the changing nature of local economies (i.e. shift patterns, location and nature of work) made it difficult for the bus network to cope with new demands. The operators' view was that historically the fares in Edinburgh have been low and are regarded by the industry to have kept pace with inflation and risen at a lower rate than the price of petrol.

There are no interventions in the Leith area by the local authority due to this view and because other areas in the city were perceived to have a greater need for subsidised bus links. The local authority stated that they do not target services geographically or by sections in the community. The basic approach was described thus:

> the actions we take are generalised and focus on the proximity to the network as a whole so that in terms of broad brush the commercial network in Leith is such that we do not ... intervene at all in that particular part of the city (City of Edinburgh Council).

There is, however, recognition by both operators and the local authority that for some sections of the community the network could never be dense enough (especially for the elderly or infirm). Operators' views of the constraints faced in the area are principally viewed in terms of rising levels of car ownership and parking problems that can in turn affect service reliability. Flexitime was cited by one operator as having a negative impact on services because this made it difficult to gauge the demand for services. In Leith this was not regarded as a problem.

There was a feeling expressed by the local authority that there may possibly be some real exclusion in areas where car ownership in the majority of the population is fairly high and where, as a result, you have inadequate commercial networks:

> As a result you have very sparse commercial networks but where you have for example, an elderly population component who, because of that situation, don't have the frequent or close public transport system and I think, for example, of a great swathe of ... inner Edinburgh ... you think of the sort of Marchmont, Sciennes, Grange area where the social exclusion is probably on the basis of age and inability to drive and not the commercial network being somewhat sparser than it used to be. Most of our SIPS have quite reasonable bus services but ... there are pockets ... one thinks of, for example, Calder's housing area out on Calder Road where because of geography it's at the end of a network ... within the scheme itself I suspect there's at the very least a feeling of exclusion when the bus operators withdraw (City of Edinburgh Council).

The commercial provision of services does, however, cause problems for example at weekends and particularly on Sundays, when levels of patronage are low. Operators look for on average a 15 per cent rate of return on their investment on commercial routes but this can be reduced to around 10 per cent on subsidised services. This concern for an adequate return on investment has resulted in a refocusing of activity on major corridors so that services can be run at a higher frequency, yet there is also recognition by operators of the benefits of cross-subsidisation through their network in terms of different patronage levels on routes. The focus on corridors is viewed as an essential step in order to increase their business. The consequences of this activity for areas within the city generally and Leith are recognised. Operators in Edinburgh agree that public transport cannot serve every area and that there is a need to pick out corridors, although it is also recognised that there are problems in selecting the main corridors with the highest number of passengers. First Edinburgh, for example, have consolidated routes in the city centre onto five routes in the city that have Greenways:

> There are some communities that have lost ... bus services as a result. LRT have done something slightly similar in the sort of ongoing programme of what they see as network improvements but marginally profitable communities lose out. I mean it's actually very unpredictable I think and again this is a consequence of the fact that it's done on a commercial basis rather than some sort of public needs planning (City of Edinburgh Council).

Adjustments to routes had recently been made by Lothian Buses as a result of major new developments in the Port of Leith. This was principally in the form of new low floor bus service serving Ocean Terminal and the Scottish Executive. As a representative from Lothian Buses put it:

> I suppose one of the principal very recent developments in the port area is changes to our service 22, which was just in March of this year, because it is the first instance in the urban network of our introduction of a style of operation which is not uncommon elsewhere ... we are seeing some encouraging reaction to that from people, the premise being that with a very high frequency service you obviate the need for a detailed timetable. People don't worry too much about what the timetable is because they know whenever they arrive at the stop there'll be another bus there in five minutes. Obviously operating at these high frequencies requires more vehicles to be allocated to the service from the traditional pattern, I think that can lead to some consolidation so that there are other parts of the network where links are broken or resources are withdrawn or reallocated (Lothian Buses).

As a result of this process, when the network is changed there was recognition that areas would lose out but that there would be more winners than losers at the end of the adjustment to a route. A similar restructuring of routes has been undertaken by First Edinburgh, who operate a number of services that come into the city centre and then access other areas through interchange on to other services. Interestingly, the levels of service enjoyed by the more affluent areas is invariably dependent on the:

> application of commercial surpluses which are made in low income areas. It's simply the nature of business. So that's why the specific targeting of services in low income areas is not something that receives a great deal of attention because to be perfectly honest they are the most commercially buoyant and viable parts of the network (Lothian Buses).

The modal share enjoyed by bus operators in Edinburgh also makes it easier for bus companies to maintain networks.

A substantial proportion of income for operators is from commercial passengers. The contribution in terms of route support is very small. An area of concern is the fall in the numbers of concessionary trips, partly due the fact that new cohorts of older people are more likely to drive. Lothian Buses, in an attempt to counter this trend, have begun to offer their commercial fares at a significantly discounted price to those eligible for concessionary travel (this includes offering an extra month or two months on the annual ticket which is available to concessionary passengers). FirstEdinburgh operate a special fare after 9.30am (70p), as well as a weekly and monthly Travel Club ticket. This offers unlimited access across their network for those periods. They also give change, which their competitors do not do. FirstEdinburgh indicated that take up of their Travel Club tickets is 20 per cent lower in Leith than in other areas of the city. Purchase of these tickets can be made on the bus, at the post office and at their central Edinburgh office in St Andrew Square. The take-up for Travel Club tickets is larger outside the city, where people are not travelling on a regular basis.

The provision of timetable information is the responsibility of operators. Lothian Buses provide free leaflets for every service and also customised timetables for each bus stop in the network. Difficulties surrounding the provision of travel information on their new corridors was acknowledged by FirstEdinburgh, who were now seeking to produce travel information on a corridor by corridor basis. Each of the operators also have dedicated travel information telephone systems and service changes are advertised. First Edinburgh have experimented with providing travel information surgeries at libraries on the south side of Edinburgh but this has not been undertaken in Leith.

Policy Developments

The City of Edinburgh Council works closely with the Social Inclusion Partnership areas in the city and has taken an innovative step to assessing the problem of social exclusion and transport through the establishment of a Transport Task Force. The Task Force has contributed to the development of the local transport strategy (LTS) for the city. The LTS was felt by the local authority broadly to reflect the transport priorities for the city, despite the perception that may be held by particular groups that there may not be much on social exclusion contained within the document.

The Task Force is a grouping consisting of representatives from several departments in the City Council (including Education, City Development, Social Work and other external agencies representing the disabled) and essentially stemmed from a community care background. The grouping does not involve the unemployed or other groups who would consider themselves as excluded, and has focused not only on issues associated with older people and people with disabilities but has also looked at other areas of exclusion. The Task Force has recently produced a report that recognises the broader transport needs of particular users and seeks to pursue a greater integration of transport services provided by education, social work and community transport provided by community groups. The ultimate goal is to develop in a more planned and programmed way as an adjunct to the conventional bus network, possibly a dial-a-bus type service with flexible routing.

Support is provided by the local authority for dial-a-bus, community transport and transport services provided by education and social work departments of the local authority. An emerging view, but not necessarily a shared one, for community transport in Leith is the need for a strategy that addresses all community transport for the city as one respondent indicated:

> There are social car schemes that operate in the city, they tend to be located either with churches or particular voluntary organisations and particular client groups. They have a network of car schemes and there's no ... strategy of delivering social car schemes in the city but they are very ... isolated and ad hoc and I don't have a list of them, I don't even know where they all are, I mean I know of a few ... and the same with minibus operators in the community voluntary sector, there's not ... a centralised list so I don't actually know ... how many there are, so that's our view of how we provide community transport (Lothian Community Transport Services).

LCTs have also started to look at providing feeder services for bus route corridors in rural areas of Midlothian. There are also possibilities that this model of transport provision could be extended into urban areas, but no discussion on this has yet taken place.

To date, the feeling within the local authority was that more effort had been put into linking the location of crossing facilities with bus stops, looking at interchange facilities and identifying a programme of bus boarders around the city. The recent Public Transport Fund bid by the city had included an element of bus boarder work in Leith to enable people to gain access more easily to low floor vehicles. The local authority did not target investment into transport infrastructure where particular forms of social exclusion was known to exist. The view was expressed that:

> ... there are undoubtedly some sectors of the community that one might assume to be excluded that perhaps we don't put a lot of, at least haven't to date put a lot of, effort into and they're the ... sectors of the community, for example unemployed ... We don't, for example, have a targeted ... list of census districts where ... exclusions are a particular issue and then gone geographically and tied it down, although again our public transport fund bid for the first time has looked at the whole issue of social exclusion and has targeted the design of the bid in particular to link jobs with the south Edinburgh areas where unemployment is particularly high and it builds on the work that we've done on social exclusion in Edinburgh ... we haven't been at it long enough to have a ... clear set of strategies that we adopt each time so we are ... developing that and I think the trigger for that is very much the ... social exclusion work that we did for the Interim LTS (City of Edinburgh Council).

A list of criteria does exist for assisting the decision-making process for tendered services, but it was found that the criteria could be applied to justify almost any type of decision for a tendered route. The indications are also that decisions to offer tendered routes can also be influenced by the amount of political and public pressure that is brought to bear in particular circumstances. Most subsidised services, however, are on the basis of providing bus travel for the elderly to shops, social facilities and hospitals. The journey to work does not feature significantly in decisions for tendered services.

Ticketing initiatives were seen to be an extremely important area of activity, but the current emphasis is clearly geared towards modal shift. Concessionary travel, although an important part of a commercial operator's business, is declining in terms of trips and is also currently constrained in terms of the classes of people that use it (i.e. women over 60, men over 65 and disabled people). FirstEdinburgh and Lothian Buses had worked together to establish Transfare, a scheme that allowed passengers with one operator's season ticket to use a service run by the other operator. An inter-ticketing scheme has also been put forward by the South of Scotland Transport Partnership. The emphasis within the scheme is modal shift, although potentially it is anticipated that it could have an impact on travel by the socially excluded. Targeted cross-subsidisation was identified as an area that the local authority would be interested to pursue to help ensure adequate service levels on routes at particular times during the day or to help underpin the development of new routes. Yet it was also recognised that it is very difficult to specify a basis on which interventions should occur on tendered routes for example:

> ... should we support those services which very few people are travelling on and obviously the ... cost per journey ends up being quite a lot. On the other hand, you might argue that we should pay for those services on which more people want to travel, but then those are the ones that maybe the bus company should be doing commercially so I think it's quite difficult how you intervene (City of Edinburgh Council).

There is clearly scope within new ticketing arrangements for targeted cross-subsidisation to be discussed on a geographical or route basis.

Quality Partnerships were viewed as a way in which public transport services could be developed and targeted. Indeed, one operator felt that more thought could be put into the 'pump-priming' of services, possibly as part of a Quality Partnership to assist with the development of new service. Quality Partnerships are viewed favourably by the industry but there was general feeling that it had to be a real partnership, with the local authority playing a central role. Operators, however, felt that approval mechanisms for Quality Partnership agreements are cumbersome.

Quality Contracts, it was felt, could be made more attractive to local authorities if they could specify every aspect of the service, although it was felt that there were too many barriers to implementation and that a 21-month period between going into the tender process and actually implementing a Quality Contract was seen by the local authority as being too long. The view of operators in Edinburgh is that these will ruin the industry. One operator commented that franchising creates a situation that is time-specific in terms of the length of the franchise. From the operators' view this places additional costs on the operation of the service which they will need to recover over the franchise period. The local authority did view the Quality Contract as a way in which a local authority could specify the requirement for a network to be established and because bus routes in Edinburgh are quite profitable that a degree of cross-subsidisation could be possible.

Intervention of some kind was seen by the local authority as desirable given current experiences of market operation:

> I think the lesson is that left to its own devices the market will concentrate on those high, those corridors that are seen as high volume passengers and will leave the other areas relatively unserved (City of Edinburgh Council).

One operator stated that they had a strong view about historical network effects in a commercial environment and that if a slightly different approach were taken then there would possibly be a smaller network:

> I mean, every day 150,000 or 200,000 depend on us to get them to work, to get them to school, to get them home again and we cannot just take a blank map and start drawing straight lines all over it and expect that to be 1) deliverable in any kind of sensible timeframe or 2) viewed as a big step forward by most existing users because there is a dialogue going on. Not only do we make commercial choices about what the revenue maximising network will be, although we don't go for a revenue maximising network here in this company, because if we did the network would be significantly smaller but the network which balances adequate revenue and market share with maximising ridership (Lothian Buses).

There was evidence that the local authority were beginning to discuss internally ways in which the gaps in commercial service operation could be filled geographically and at particular times of day but there was also a desire not to duplicate those services that were already in existence:

> ... there's no point at all in having ... organisations with, in my view, organisations with minibuses ... plodding the same sort of corridor that mainstream buses are, particularly if over a period you've moved to truly accessibly mainstream public transport you can actually get to ... There will always be a core of people for whom you have to make special provision and that's given constrained budgets ... where we should be targeting. Duplication ... simply isn't in anybody's interest and there is a substantial amount that remains to be done ... but again we've been thinking about that lately to try and fill the gaps geographically or at quiet times of day or for those people who can't use mainstream public transport or at least need help to get to mainstream public transport. So our ... basic philosophy I guess would always be make sure that the ... first stab that you end up with as mainstream public ... then

make sure that you target those areas and sections of the community that you need to … (City of Edinburgh Council).

Community transport was recognised as having an important role to play but no coherent strategy was in place in terms of the relationship with the LTS. The City of Edinburgh Council are currently discussing the possibility of devising a community transport strategy that 'nests' within the Local Transport Strategy. There is, though, currently no vehicle for forming links with the voluntary sector. Certainly this view was taken by a representative of the community transport sector in Edinburgh:

> The big issue for us in terms of Edinburgh is that there's no strategy in place for the development or the provision of community transport services. There's no understanding as to how or why the council supports different initiatives at different levels in different places. There are community groups that are funded to one level and other community groups a mile or two away that are funded to a different level providing perhaps different services and there's no understanding in the council as to how or why that's happened and what we're trying to get is a clear understanding that if the council's going to buy into the voluntary transport sector it knows how it does it, why it does it and where it's going with that development (Lothian Community Transport Services).

Involvement by the community transport sector was viewed positively in principle by operators but there was a concern expressed about the amount of funding that would be required to get new initiatives started.

The service route concept is an idea that has been considered by the Council a number of times. Typically this is a service that would operate at off-peak times and although relatively slow compared to conventional forms of public transport service would offer a personalised service that could be targeted at neighbourhood communities, health centres and sheltered housing blocks. Specifically it would be aimed at people who placed a high value on door-to-door travel. This concept had been discussed when the Council extended the dial-a-bus service, the idea being to widen the eligibility criteria in terms of social exclusion. The taxi-card scheme (discounted taxi travel) is another way in which door to door transport could be provided to other excluded groups as long as the eligibility criteria were widened to other groups beyond people with disabilities. Other specialised transport services had not been discussed in the context of social exclusion. The car club concept, for example, is currently only offered in relatively wealthy parts of the city (Marchmont, Sciennes, Bruntsfield and Merchiston) due to higher levels of car ownership.

Land-use planning is regarded as extremely important not only in terms of the provision of community facilities, but also in terms of the location of new employment and retail centres that could be easily served by public transport. Operators and the local authority all cited the important role of land-use planning. Operators also viewed more favourably those developments such as new housing schemes and new industrial estates where bus facilities had been incorporated into the development. FirstEdinburgh also indicated that it had become involved in planning inquiries, but these had mainly been for retail areas in these situations where developers build in facilities. These arrangements, however, do not tend to stipulate levels of service.

Peripheral Housing Estate – Castlemilk, City of Glasgow

Views of the Network

The area itself, along with other peripheral estates, is recognised as an area of low car ownership. The areas are viewed as being particularly important in terms of public transport patronage. The view expressed both by the local authority and operators was that the area is well served by public transport but that public transport could not provide a door-to-door service. FirstGlasgow and Strathclyde Passenger Transport (SPT) were not aware of any particular issues or problems in the area, but there was recognition that particularly unusual time or link requirements would always be a problem. The changing location and pattern of work for Castlemilk residents was identified as a particular issue by the Castlemilk Economic Development Agency.[1] As a result, a subsidised route supported by SPT was operated between Castlemilk and East Kilbride, an important employment area for Castlemilk residents.

The emphasis in Glasgow City Council's strategy is based on encouraging public transport and modal shift. The link between social exclusion and transport *per se* is seen as an adjunct to the main policy goal of modal shift. A number of areas are identified as impinging on social exclusion; for example, healthy transport, including the reduction of pollution and road danger and the need to encourage the use of roads for all users, including cyclists and pedestrians. The two policy objectives are not viewed as being incompatible. Public transport use is encouraged, particularly for commuting, and this policy is directed more towards those areas in the city where the more economically active sections of the population live. The Council is actively pursuing Quality Bus Corridors as part of this strategy, although some communities and retailers felt that they were detrimental to the provision of local shopping facilities. The City Council is unable to do anything about the levels of service on offer but can make services more efficient through the implementation of particular traffic management schemes. Issues surrounding public transport provision were passed on to SPT. A representative of the council stated:

> At the same time we would like to think that the improvements we are making are generally of use so that people in the peripheral estates who are coming in by bus will get the benefit of it as well. The planned bus corridors will link into these areas. We have a more direct role to play in bus transport less so for rail (Glasgow City Council).

The Council has also opened up the bus lanes to taxis in recognition of their important role in the peripheral estates. Support of services to these areas is addressed by SPT, who are responsible for filling these gaps, but the level of support is dictated by the amount of funding available. In the SPT area 90 per cent of services are commercially operated. The City Council had recently undertaken a survey of households in the city and had found that concerns about public transport service frequency and ticketing were the biggest concerns.

FirstGlasgow, Stagecoach and First Stop Travel (a smaller operator) are currently in competition for passengers in Castlemilk. A tendered service is operated by DART, funded by SPT, with a contribution from the Castlemilk Economic Development Agency. FirstGlasgow recently reviewed services in the Glasgow area in an attempt to stabilise their customer base and reverse downward trends in patronage. Once a solid platform has been established, it is their intention to then provide new public transport initiatives. As an operator they would argue that they are investing man hours and vehicles in retaining reliability rather than increasing frequency. The operator identified the patterns of demand in terms of major links to the City Centre, the East End and other links across the city to the north. The operator stated that:

> ... the links across the city are not demand-based but tend to be more based on operational efficiency. Castlemilk unusually for this company tends to have its city services, its services that served the city centre, terminating in the city centre. Most other areas of the city actually had a history of cross-city operation. More recently the destination for these – St Enochs Square – closed and that has also prompted the cross city provision (FirstGlasgow).

Links going back three or four years were reviewed following competition from Stagecoach. Stagecoach provided high frequency links (every 10 minutes) on the best city routes, one of them being a route coming into the city from Castlemilk. FirstGlasgow responded by moving to a 'like for like' service and refocused activity on major corridors.

The introduction of the Overground has meant that Castlemilk was served by both service 5 and service 75, both of which are Overground services. Both are low floor services and between them provide a five minute service frequency between Castlemilk and the city centre:

> Essentially the decision that had been taken was that there was a natural loop within Castlemilk and that service 75 and 5 could between them provide a five minute link into the city centre using that loop and every second journey would follow a route that would be deemed to be more direct and every other journey would follow a route via the Victoria Infirmary and Victoria Road (FirstGlasgow).

The 75 is a competitive service and has a lower fare structure. This is the fastest service and therefore the cheapest. Passengers have been found to favour this service because it is cheap and direct. Other services, such as the 74, provide other links but survive as a result of the core city business. The 37 and 46 provide links into the East side of city (37 goes to Milton and 46 to Easterhouse). The 46 runs half hourly and the 37 every 15 minutes and these service frequencies reflect the lower demand for these services on the other side of the city centre. The principle is essentially to protect current business:

> ... rather than use all of your strengths to cover for weaknesses, build on your strengths and have a solid platform that when it comes to dealing with the weaker services it creates a more solid core so you are building the strengths out ... In Castlemilk it was probably more straightforward than most places because they already had two or three high frequency services and it was just a matter of consolidating on those. Other niche markets ... are probably best dealt with as a second network (FirstGlasgow).

The Overground network is non-subsidised, although there is some income from student travel passes. Off-peak services are provided as a result of the high levels of usage throughout the day. Timetable information is provided for each service but the distribution of timetable information is very difficult. Information at stops is going through an improvement and is recognised as a very difficult exercise, due to service changes and vandalism.

First Stop Travel operate two commercial services in Castlemilk – the 134 and 234 (134 Govan to Castlemilk via Castlemilk Drive and 234 Govan,

Crowfoot to Castlemilk). The 134 is a 15-minute service to Menock Road where the service separates to a half service on the Menock Road. The 234 is a half hour service. Buses run from 7.50am out of Castlemilk. The last bus out of Castlemilk is 7pm. The services are targeted at a variety of users. The perception of this operator was that:

> ... the area was poorly serviced prior to us operating the service. Since then FirstGlasgow has increased its service and its reliability. They are our competitors on the road (First Stop Travel).

The operator recognised problems with timetable information and had worked with a local community group to get timetable information out through a local newspaper. The two services are profitable, with patronage being very stable. As a smaller operator they felt that they would like to operate a more frequent service but currently do not operate in the evening due to the low numbers of passengers. Concerns were voiced about competition with other larger operators who could further refocus activity on the main corridors at higher frequencies leaving smaller operators to operate in the schemes:

> ... the fear is that we will be left with the small pieces and the larger operators are left with the more lucrative parts of the service and would not be viable (First Stop Travel).

A subsidised route is provided by SPT for part of the day for a service (service 95) linking East Kilbride and Castlemilk. The service was originally supported by Glasgow Development Agency and is now supported by Castlemilk Economic Development Agency. The service is currently operated by DART. Problems had been experienced with service due to the changing pattern of use as people's working lives become established:

> The initial stages did appear to be meeting a lot of the aims and carrying a lot of passengers between Castlemilk and East Kilbride whereas as East Kilbride began to grow and there was a kind of diversity in the shift operating times it meant that the bus was becoming increasingly irrelevant ... What we've done is, we've tried, when the bus was originally established the people who were using it the bus was relevant for and as these people established their working life they would then go and get cars or make their own arrangements to get to work from other people within their office or factory or whatever so the people who were using the bus changed and the needs changed so what we've had to do is constantly monitor the service (Castlemilk Economic Development Agency).

The subsidy to run the service has been reduced from £35,000 at the start of the service's operation to a subsidy level of around £1,200. The current operator DART (a small operator) indicated that they had hoped to build up the service commercially but that the route was proving difficult to operate commercially due to gaps in the timetable:

> We've done it with one or two other services that we had a subsidy. When the subsidy ran out we were able to retain most of it commercially. This one doesn't show a lot of signs of life, it's an unusual timetable. It was an early morning journey for workers, 7.20am to Castlemilk, the next bus is after 9am so whether it's because there's a bus missing at that sort of back of eight time or not I don't know but overall the usage is, even by tendered standards, low ... I mean you would tend to think that the process ought to be that the subsidies to some extent pump priming and that once the service is there for a while and the bus service is notoriously slow to build up custom but once it's there for a while the level of usage will grow to the extent that either no subsidy or less of a subsidy's required and in the case of this one then there's no sign of any sort of increase in demand particularly (DART).

The operator commented that the service seemed to carry shoppers and pensioners although it had been designed for employment reasons. There was anecdotal evidence to suggest that once workers became established in work that they switched to private cars. The gaps in timetable and lack of publicity surrounding timetable information were cited as problematic, despite them operating a telephone information service:

> I think we would like to see a more comprehensive timetable to start with even though you're being paid for whatever you're doing and if there's gaps it's reflected in the price just in simplicity particularly non-bus users or non-users of that service knowing what it does it's a comprehensive timetable to start with. It's not well publicised in truth by either us or the PTE or CEDA and that's not just sort of advertising, it's employers knowing that there's a bus link to Castlemilk and it can offer journeys at these times, people in Castlemilk knowing that they can get to these parts of East Kilbride when they're considering job options (DART).

Nevertheless, although it was felt that there were undoubtedly opportunities, there were problems for small operators:

> For a small operator the costs are almost certainly too high. On the one hand you've got to run the investment to get the service up, on the other you're

probably seen as being predatory and competing against the established operator regardless of the differences in the product so you've got the risk of a competitive reaction from them and put those two together and it's just not worth it (DART).

Policy Developments

A strong preference was expressed for Quality Partnerships by Glasgow City Council but more regulation was favoured by SPT. The problems associated with Quality Partnerships as currently specified were that they do not cover timetabling, service frequency and route. Quality Contracts were viewed more favourably by SPT as a form of franchising but it was felt that the procedures associated with implementation were very cumbersome, for example the requirement for ministerial approval. Smaller operators may also be excluded from Quality Partnerships due to the relatively high administration and set-up costs involved in negotiating a partnership with a local authority. Franchising would also cause problems for small operators but:

> ... you would probably find that people like FirstGlasgow would, the deeper the pocket they have the more they can throw about (through cross-subsidisation of routes) we see it now. They come in with the big muscle on it and start slapping us about (First Stop Travel).

CEDA took a view that Partnerships should be viewed as a way in which local authorities with transport operators could identify new market opportunities as new employment opportunities are established. There was a recognition that there was a need to respond effectively to changes in the local economy and new job opportunities was an important factor in terms of being able to change timetables and frequencies in a way that would enhance the contribution that public transport could make:

> I think if it was easier to change the times of the routes or the times that the bus actually runs that would really help ... as new opportunities come up. For example we had an employer who won a significant contract and were looking for quite an influx of labour, I think it was about 50 or 60 new members of staff. Now had we been able to change the times quickly to fit in with that we might have been able to fill half if not all of the jobs ... I feel that the transport has to act just as quickly because without it basically the clients can't get the work (Castlemilk Economic Development Agency).

A community transport organisation in Castlemilk had tried to establish services and discussions with CEDA had been held, but a problem with recruiting enough volunteer drivers was identified. A respondent stated:

> It's difficult to get the people to run something that's going to be effective or efficient or to meet the same sort of standards of buses as they are, but we are discussing with community transport about arranging things but as yet nothing has really come out (Castlemilk Economic Development Agency).

Subsidised taxis had been looked at to help people access jobs in East Kilbride but it had been concluded that the costs would be too high and that it would be very difficult to 'police' how they were used:

> Taxis were too expensive. We've looked at the cost of the taxis and we felt there was a point when … perhaps we could subsidise taxis but we were … only dealing with three or four passengers on the buses at the time that we were looking at this, and the cost was something like £6 for a taxi between here and East Kilbride, how much of that would we decide to subsidise, how do we police that in terms of making sure that that run goes on and that if the run does go on how do we know the figures of people that are? There's also the issue of taxis. When I spoke to the Passenger Transport fellow he said there were incidents where underground trains go off and there's maybe four or five people travelling on between two stations, they put on a taxi and all of a sudden it goes up to 16, 17 people turning up for taxis, people who would not have otherwise bothered if it appeared on their doorstep and I felt perhaps that might have been the case here (Castlemilk Economic Development Agency).

Financial exclusion was an important issue identified by Castlemilk Economic Development Agency. Loans to assist with the purchase of motor vehicles to help with travel to work were potentially problematic in terms of the banking sectors' concerns over repayments. For residents who had just started work the Agency were currently able to pay for their Zone Card and they would be reimbursed when the recipient had received their first pay cheque. Other options such as car pooling had been investigated but this had not been taken any further. CEDA were exploring the development of links with employers who run workers' buses.

Free Standing Town – Coatbridge, North Lanarkshire

Views of the Network

The local authority for the area, North Lanarkshire Council, although concerned with modal shift and the Road Traffic Reduction Act in terms of encouraging public transport use in its area, also recognised the importance of public transport for those households who have no car or very limited access to the car. Social exclusion had received attention in the Local Transport Strategy for the area and this had involved developing partnerships within the Council (Education and Social Work), SPT, and the local enterprise company.

The Council indicated that the main problems facing the area are due to the dispersal of activities. The population in the area is spread over seven large towns and many smaller local communities and the result is that:

> ... there's no single urban centre that anyone wants to go to and a lot of the public transport network reflects the kind of West of Scotland dominance of Glasgow and this kind of greater conurbation there. There's links between our larger settlements, the kind of Bellshill, Motherwell, Coatbridge, Airdrie, but there's very few links from the smaller villages in, that form part of an integrated network. The bus operators ... larger operators are focussing on main corridors which don't serve the bulk of the population. Smaller operators have been asked to kind of fill in the gaps from the smaller villages and outlying housing areas but in terms of ticketing and timetabling and information the whole system's very fragmented (North Lanarkshire Council).

The SPT provide subsidised services for the area accounting for approximately £900,000 of subsidy; this accounts for approximately 30 per cent of the total budget available for subsidised transport in the SPT area, but this does not meet all needs and provides:

> ... a patchwork of bus services in Lanarkshire which is no way the ideal and their hands [SPT] are tied in the same way our hands are tied in trying to change that, given the way the commercial bus operators are allowed to work and the kind of lack of legislative tools we've got to address that and the lack of a budget as well a subsidised bus budget is very limited (North Lanarkshire Council).

Lanarkshire is viewed as an extremely competitive market by operators, more so than the city market. It has many operators providing many local links. Minibus operators provide links locally and to the city and absorb some of the demand at main periods during the day. These services typically run from 8am to 6pm on Mondays to Saturdays. FirstGlasgow have recently introduced a network similar to the Overground in order to:

... identify the strong demand areas and tie these together in a fashion that will encourage those customers to stay and new customers to come in. At the minute the area has three longer 10-minute services backed up by a few 15-minute links. Because the complexity of the network had to be reduced, some of the links as a result of running fewer routes were broken; this was seen as way of continuing the quality of service set against the type of competition over the main sections that we were facing ... some of the best core business at the best core times is being competed for very strongly and the expectation is that as the old incumbent that the people who are there at night and who are there on Sunday are us, but these are not supported, these still have to be paid for from the element of the stronger parts of the day and the stronger elements of these routes (FirstGlasgow).

It was noted that the issue in the evening is possibly associated with fact that there are lots of small operators on the street prior to this time, but then they stop running at 6pm. FirstGlasgow operate two services in Coatbridge that run from the early morning to late evening (the 201 from 5.30am to 11pm Monday to Saturday and 9am to 11pm on Sundays and the Glasgow service 6am to 11pm Monday to Saturdays and 8am to 10.30pm Sundays. These services typically run at a 10 minute daytime frequency and a half hourly frequency in the evening. The operator also stated that they run frequent and direct links from most other North Lanarkshire towns and Coatbridge. Interchange is possible but many trips are direct and there is a strong preference for direct bus service, although it was recognised that links with Cumbernauld were difficult. The view taken by SPT was that in Coatbridge the bus network was integrated but the large operators had effectively 'walked away' from the area and, combined with the closure of the Airdrie bus garage, had resulted in the current situation. The small operators were viewed as a problem in terms of lack of timetabling and reliability and this was compounded by the lack of resources that the Traffic Commissioners have to monitor operator behaviour:

The bus operators like the flexibility you know to cut services that 42 days' notice gives them, they like being unanswerable to anybody except the traffic commissioner. As long as they don't do anything really bizarrely stupid, the traffic commissioner will tend not to do a great deal, it's the facts you know, it's unfortunately the facts, it's the commercial bus world and it was disappointing you know, the ministers in Scotland made their comment that the bus operators should realise their social obligations you know in terms of quality partnership and I think if you ask a local authority officer or an SPT officer what social obligations the bus operators have got they'd say very few if any and the bottom line budget-wise, that's what the bus operator's looking for (North Lanarkshire Council).

In Coatbridge there was a particular problem of bus services running along a corridor from Airdrie to Coatbridge and then on to Glasgow which made it very difficult for people in Coatbridge to access new employment centres at EuroCentral and the Bellshill Industrial Park. Car use was seen by many as the only viable mode of transport to access these new employment centres. The problem of public transport trying to meet new shift patterns was noted as a particular problem for residents in Coatbridge:

> We're moving away from the traditional manufacturing to modern manufacturing and assembly and information technology type stuff so your shift patterns are changing from very big workforces coming out ... a morning shift and an evening shift to three or four shifts a day, it makes it more difficult. There are, well, a few things we're trying to do. The SPT in their kind of public transport role are looking at, they've done a project in South Lanarkshire in terms of the rural transport trying to link school bus services, community transport, the dial-a-bus and such, the idea of getting the services to perform different roles so that you can make the best use of the budget. The next rural transport study they're going to do is in North Lanarkshire (North Lanarkshire Council).

The local authority was very keen for the role of community transport to be developed in delivering services within the area. This would involve breaking down the barriers between community transport, school transport and subsidised services.

The local authority essentially viewed the focus of activity on corridors as market failure. An example provided was the Airdrie to Coatbridge corridor where all services are provided by one large operator. Services to the corridor are provided by other operators. As a result people from areas not on the corridor will have to change and pay two bus fares:

> If they can afford a car they've got a car in a lot of cases, particularly in the smaller villages where a car's essential, you are looking at the elderly folk, the children, unemployed folks, people going to hospital and, such the ones who can't actually drive and they're now required to spend a lot more time, a lot more money taking a bus. It's not a good way ahead (North Lanarkshire Council).

The local authority shared SPT concerns about ticketing arrangements and travel information in the area.

FirstGlasgow revealed that the company were currently finalising behavioural undertakings with the Office of Fair Trading following the purchase of Strathclyde Buses in 1996. The behavioural undertakings mean that the company cannot increase fares at a level greater than the retail price index. FirstGlasgow indicated that any fare increase has a negative elasticity; in other words, for the company to stand still it actually has to grow patronage at the same rate as the negative elasticity. FirstGlasgow has also moved towards simplifying fare structures as well as simplifying the network. This has resulted in the introduction of an off-peak return in the city area of £1.50, against a standard fare of £1 (approximately). A transfer ticket (£1.30) which entitles the user to board two buses within 90 minutes has also been introduced – prior to that taking two journeys meant paying two single fares. The new ticketing represents a fare saving (equivalent to 30 per cent discount) and sales of the ticket are increasing. The company also have weekly, four-weekly, 10-weekly and annual tickets. This originally operated on a complex zonal basis but this has now been redesigned to include the city area, and then areas beyond on a £7, £9, and £11 basis (dependent on the number of zones that are crossed). For this process it was admitted that to some extent *there were winners and losers* (FirstGlasgow). In Lanarkshire there is the additional benefit of an £11 ticket being available for £10. The scheme has been designed to encourage patronage and has resulted in a shift from a 5–6 per cent passenger loss to a 1–2 per cent growth.

Policy Development

The local authority for the area are continuing to look at the role of community transport. This would involve breaking down the barriers between community transport, school transport and subsidised services. The level of subsidy available for services was viewed as problematic in the sense that it had created a patchwork of services. The SPT and local authority are both in favour of more regulation to counter the competitive behaviour of operators.

Quality partnerships were viewed favourably by the bus industry but North Lanarkshire Council and the SPT felt that it can only work if operators continue to meet their commitments and there was a perception that little could be done in terms of policing these agreements. A form of franchising was the favoured option:

> They can't deliver a level of certainty that a quality contract or some form of franchising would allow, and ... the rail services are franchised, the bus services in London are franchised, it can work and we're required to jump through dozens of hoops over a space of maybe seven years just to come up with a quality contract. No, that's not the best way forwards, is a fair way to say it (North Lanarkshire Council).

There was also concern about how it could be judged that a Partnership had failed. As in other areas there was some concern expressed about the cumbersome nature of the procedures that were potentially required to establish a Quality Contract:

> Then you've got the process by which they've got to set up a contract. And speaking to the folks in SPT it'll take you two years from start to finish to go from ... we need to set up a contract to being in a position to deliver the contract and that's two years wherein your non-working commercially operated bus services are still running after the three years for the partnership, perhaps being allowed to run its time plus the lead-up time for the partnership, a year/two years so you are running seven years of not delivering services to the public before you can actually go and run that contract service (North Lanarkshire Council).

Franchising was seen by the local authority and SPT as extremely desirable method of providing public transport services. The local authority representative discussed a potentially viable option in the form of an area based franchising operation consisting of nested operations in different areas of operation:

> It's complex but I think if it's done fairly a bus operator gets 10 money-making routes on the understanding they provide 15 social routes to a minimum level (North Lanarkshire Council).

The minimum level would be a specified standard. The perception was that a franchised operation would overcome many difficulties:

> I think its FirstBus and the Overground ... they're developing the corridors, that's a partnership and SPT signed up to it very soon after it was launched. There were complaints that the buses on the Overground corridor had been taken away from the peripheral housing schemes in Glasgow, services had been cut there to provide the new Overground services, SPT was left having to find a hole in its subsidised bus budget to put these back in. A franchise could have avoided that (North Lanarkshire Council).

SPT, the local authority and operators agreed that the design and location of new residential areas and industrial estates were considered to be an extremely important issue if public transport use was to be encouraged and operators were to be encouraged into housing schemes. There was a clear need for developers to build in as many advantages as possible:

... growing a bus service is extremely difficult from scratch as you put all your costs up front and in that circumstance revenue has to follow very quickly. Changing people's habits is really the great challenge (FirstGlasgow).

Taxis were identified as a flexible mode of transport, but their role in terms of meeting transport policy objectives had not really been developed in North Lanarkshire.

Conclusions

Evidence from these interviews with local authorities and transport operators clearly indicates the need for more targeting of resources geographically or at particular groups. Local authorities in Scotland have only just begun to recognise the nature of exclusion and the potentially wide-ranging effects that transport can play in creating exclusion. Local Transport Strategies produced by the three local authorities (and discussed in Chapter 3) reflect the degree to which authorities had thought through issues related to transport and social exclusion.

The use, or proposed use, of quality bus corridors has resulted in concerns that housing areas adjacent to these routes will suffer from lower levels of provision, as services are increasingly concentrated on these corridors. The key issue in the future may be how these local populations can access these transport corridors. When combined with service withdrawal or the realignment of bus service routes, it is likely that areas and communities with low car ownership will experience a reduction in the level and quality of public of transport service available to them. Community transport operators have identified this growing service gap and a need for a coordinated approach amongst the many groups and other local authority departments (Education and Social Work) providing community transport.

The main operators in each area are able to cross-subsidise services to ensure a regular service throughout the day. There were concerns, especially in Glasgow, that competition from smaller operators could weaken the ability of bus operators to cross-subsidise. The provision of subsidised services and concessions paid for by local authorities and the PTE is fraught with difficulties, reflecting a wider concern that it is difficult to target resources geographically or at particular groups in the current operational environment. Moreover, it was felt that it can prove to be difficult to justify the targeting of these resources at the expense of other groups and areas.

Note

1   The Castlemilk Economic Development Agency (CEDA), originally established under the New Life for Urban Scotland Partnership, has now developed independently of the Partnership. CEDA has developed a whole range of services beyond a job training function but has now moved into the development of other services associated with social inclusion and the voluntary sector. The organisation has identified a range of barriers to accessing jobs and employment opportunities these included both child care and transport to areas where job opportunities lay.

Chapter 7

Where Next?

Introduction

Transport policy is faced with a dilemma that needs to be urgently addressed. The nature of transport disadvantage and the process of exclusion has prompted a debate of about the shape of transport systems. As we know social exclusion reflects the existence of barriers which make it difficult or impossible for people to participate fully in society (Social Exclusion Unit, 1998). However, the process of social exclusion and the relationship with transport is little understood by local authorities. It is these authorities who regularly intervene in the local transport market to subsidise public transport services that are socially necessary (Hine and Mitchell, 2001; Sinclair et al., 2001). In previous chapters the nature of transport disadvantage and how it impacts of the accessibility of goods and services has been identified . We have also seen the way in which operators are responding to the challenges of operating in a commercial environment. In Chapter 1 a number of key questions that relate to the direction of UK transport policy were identified. These questions are:

- how is the link between transport and social exclusion characterised;
- what policy mechanisms and practices are appropriate in different circumstances;
- what are the implications of the social exclusion debate for the delivery and organisation of transport policy?

How is the Link between Transport and Social Exclusion Characterised?

Although, the link between transport and social exclusion had been widely recognised (Barry, 1998; Pacione, 1995), a paucity of data on the issue meant that the subtle relationship between transport and social exclusion could not be fully appreciated (Church et al., 1999). Nonetheless, transport disadvantage can exaggerate social exclusion further or help initiate the process of exclusion. It is clear that, despite the lack of agreement that exists when seeking to define social exclusion, there are patterns of transport access that result in differences in levels of mobility between genders, income groups, tenure groups and people living in different types of areas where public transport networks are in decline and poorly served.

In this book findings indicate clearly that women, the elderly and people with health problems experience difficulties accessing transport. Regular car access is largely the preserve of high income earners. Those on lower incomes tend to use the bus and walk. The consequence of this is that those with good car access manage to access local facilities with lower average journey times. In other words, there is a greater tendency for men and those on higher incomes to access facilities more quickly. For those who cannot access these facilities quickly and who rely on lifts and public transport, more planning of daily activities is required. As Church et al. (1999) have noted, the implications of longer journey times and the lack of access to the private car have an impact on the nature of time/space organisation within households. This also has to be viewed in terms of the nature of time/space organisation of facilities and the opportunities that individuals have in accessing these facilities.

What Policy Mechanisms and Practices are Appropriate in Different Circumstances?

The literature supports the assertion that there is a clear role for transport to facilitate access to the areas of social activity where participation is considered to be indicative of social inclusion. An increasing knowledge and awareness of the potential barriers has led to the development of policies and approaches designed to limit the impact of such barriers upon public transport usage. Indeed, the analysis of data in Chapters 4 and 5 clearly indicates that improved transport could result in significant changes in access to goods and services. The debate about 'scatters' and 'clusters' as discussed in Chapter 1 is particularly relevant here. It is not always the case that the excluded can be found in clusters or particular areas; they may also be found in scatters across time and space. This means that certain policies are more amenable to the area-based type of problem than to the individual or scatter problem. This needs to be recognised more readily when designing policy.

There are a number of policy interventions that can be introduced to improve conditions. These interventions include:

• targeting of subsidies and concessions;

- coordination and monitoring of public transport services;
- coordination of community and specialised transport operations;
- enhanced fares and ticketing agreements;
- provision for public transport in new developments;
- provision of cycling and pedestrian infrastructure;
- non-transport solutions.

Targeting Subsidies and Concessions

This study found limited use of reduced fare schemes by respondents in the household survey. Further analysis also indicated that for those on lower incomes, a greater proportion spend over £2.40 on their fares in a typical week when compared with other higher income groups. The increased targeting of subsidies and concessions in favour of transport-disadvantaged groups, such as those on low incomes, requires the development of clear criteria and mechanisms to underpin those decisions to intervene. Targeted subsidies exist in the form of concessionary fares or budget passes. Concessions are most often granted to the elderly, registered disabled and schoolchildren, although policies vary between local transport providers. Budget passes are provided to the frequent traveller in the form of multi-journey or multi-modal passes. There is clearly scope for concessionary travel, if monitored appropriately, to be widened to groups other than the elderly and disabled, where access to affordable public transport is an issue. The use of subsidies and concessions in this way will:

- improve mobility of the transport disadvantaged;
- contribute to the reduction in travel costs for those on low incomes, particularly when interchange is involved;
- possibly generate more travel on public transport amongst the transport disadvantaged;
- maintain particular transport links and meet special transport requirements.

The current use of subsidies and concessions, however, reflects a wider problem that, in the current operational environment, it is very difficult for local authorities to target resources geographically or at particular groups, and potentially even more difficult to justify the targeting of those resources at the expense of other areas and groups whose experiences of the transport system may be similar. This also raises the issue that transport operators should tackle the issue of fares for lower income groups.

Arguably, public transport subsidies can redistribute income to the less well off and improve the mobility of the transport disadvantaged. The view emerging from evidence collected in this study is that subsidies in the form of tendered services have an important role to play in maintaining particular public transport links and meeting special requirements. It is clear, however, that more could be done in terms of developing criteria to help underpin decisions made to intervene. A clear problem is that decisions to offer tendered routes in particular areas can be influenced by the amount of political and public pressure brought to bear. There was, however, recognition of the problems associated with developing mechanisms aimed to improve the targeting of route support. It is clear that this issue needs to be addressed within the context of future proposals for enhanced ticketing arrangements between operators, so that targeted cross-subsidisation can occur on particular routes and/or commercial routes. It may be possible for subsidies and concessions to be used in a similar way. Targeted cross-subsidisation was identified as an area that transport authorities would be interested in pursuing in order to help ensure adequate service levels on routes at particular times during the day, or to help underpin the development of new routes. Yet it was also recognised that it is very difficult to specify a basis on which interventions should occur on tendered routes. For example, should support be provided to fund services on which very few people are travelling where the cost per journey is high?

Coordination and Monitoring of Public Transport Services

Evidence from this study indicates that there is a clear need to coordinate and monitor services so that poor transport provision and the resultant inaccessibility, which can create social exclusion, are minimised. This responsibility should fall equally on transport operators and local authorities. Women, the elderly, the disabled and those on low incomes are more likely to suffer from a reduction in opportunities to access goods and services where access by the public transport system is weak (in terms of longer journey times, and isolated destinations that are not well served by public transport). Coordination and better management should:

- ensure desired levels of service;
- provide responsive public transport;
- enhance the services provided by small operators and their methods of operation;

- enhance the status of adaptations to network infrastructure through the packaging of service developments and improvements.

Studies have emphasised the role of coordinated services in terms of the better management and coordination of specialised services with the regular transport service as an efficient and effective means of widening access for previously excluded passengers. The benefits of better coordination are a more fully accessible bus services, financial savings, improved quality, better bus service patronage, more professional tendering, centralised vehicle management, and normalisation.

During the course of the interviews with transport providers, evidence of operators not producing up-to-date timetable information was found. In all case study areas, evidence of the withdrawal of services and a reorganisation of the commercial routes of operators was also identified. More monitoring of these trends and an evaluation of their impact is required. In particular, there was also a recognition that there was a need to respond effectively to changes in the local economy. New job opportunities were an important factor in terms of the ability to change timetables and frequencies in a way that would enhance the contribution that public transport could make to the journey to work.

The transport authorities interviewed in this study favoured some form of franchising: a) in situations where market failure or the commercial behaviour of operators had resulted in the withdrawal of services; and/or b) for all services to ensure that routes could not be changed and adjusted at short notice and that timetabling information, service frequency and fares were controlled. Operators, however, felt that franchising would place additional costs on the operation of a service because they would need to recover the cost of the operation over the franchise period.

Intervention to ensure that the continued concentration of commercial services on corridors did not leave significant network gaps was identified as a particular instance in which franchising could be used. It was also clear from discussions based around Quality Partnerships and Quality Contracts that there was a need for a new approach. Although operators and local authorities were largely in favour of Quality Partnerships, there was a recognition that they would only work if an operator continued to provide the desired level of service. This was matched by a desire from the transport authorities for some degree of control over fares and service frequency. Small operators, on the other hand, felt that they were excluded from Quality Partnership discussions because of the relatively high administrative and set-up costs associated with them.

For franchising to work, there was the recognition that it had to be flexible, not administratively cumbersome and that it needed to provide a mechanism for new market opportunities to be identified. In particular, there was also a recognition that there was a need to respond effectively to changes in the local economy. New job opportunities were an important factor in terms of being able to change timetables and frequencies in a way that would enhance the contribution that public transport could make to the journey to work.

Coordination of Community and Specialised Transport Operations

There is a growing recognition of the broader transport needs of particular users and of the need for local authorities to pursue a greater integration of publicly-funded transport services provided by education, social work and community transport offered by community groups and specialist transport providers. Although there was an awareness of community transport schemes in the locality, respondents were unable to use these schemes, principally due to the eligibility criteria in place.

This development is seen primarily as an adjunct to the conventional bus network, although the idea seems to be at a very formative stage in the public and voluntary sector. There are, however, examples of community transport providers seeking to develop feeder services onto bus route corridors and local authorities starting to discuss how gaps in commercial operation can be filled, although there is a strong desire not duplicate those services that are already in existence. Community transport was recognised as having an important role to play but no coherent strategy was in place in terms of the relationship with the LTS objectives in any local authority area.

The further development and coordination of community transport operations would require the breaking down of barriers between community transport, school transport and subsidised services. Increased coordination of transport by transport authorities, funded by the public and voluntary sector, will:

- develop links between transport services provided by education, social work and community transport groups;
- provide a network that operates on a transport need basis without duplicating the commercial network;
- assist with the development of feeder services to commercial bus corridors;
- provide an efficient way in which access to transport can be widened to previously excluded passengers;

- provide transport links, which would otherwise not be commercially viable, for access to new employment opportunities.

Evidence from this study points to a need for a closer examination of specialised transport services. The provision of specialised services relates to a number of areas and improvements. The recommendations from this study are that targeted, demand-responsive transport services can be provided through:

- subsidised and concessionary travel for taxis;
- car schemes or car clubs that can be provided either commercially or through the voluntary sector;
- extended dial-a-bus schemes, where issues of efficiency and cost criteria can be met in light of available alternatives;
- provision of service routes for those groups that place a high value on door to door travel, and importantly for all these services;
- widened eligibility criteria to accommodate particular local needs.

Taxis are often considered to be a costly mode of travel. However, the concept of a shared taxi scheme and the provision of taxi cards are two methods of reducing the costs of travel by taxi. Subsidised taxis had been looked at to help people access jobs in East Kilbride, but it had been concluded that the costs would be too high and that it would be very difficult to 'police' how they were used. The taxi card scheme (discounted taxi travel) is another way in which door-to-door transport could be provided to other excluded groups, as long as the eligibility criteria were widened to other groups beyond people with disabilities. In Castlemilk other options, such as car pooling, had been investigated, but this had not been taken any further. In Edinburgh, the car club concept, for example, is currently only offered in relatively wealthy parts of the city (Marchmont, Sciennes, Bruntsfield and Merchiston). In Castlemilk, links were also being explored with employers who run workers' buses.

The service route concept places priority on bringing the bus service as close as possible to the residents. These schemes are generally considered to be a cost-effective and efficient means of promoting independent travel amongst the mobility impaired. Typically, a service route would operate at off-peak times and, although relatively slow compared to conventional forms of public transport, would offer a personalised service that could be targeted at neighbourhood communities, health centres and sheltered housing blocks. This could be aimed at people who placed a high value on door-to-door travel. The

City of Edinburgh Council had considered such a concept a number of times and it had been discussed when the Council extended the dial-a-bus service, the idea being to widen the eligibility criteria in terms of social exclusion.

Enhanced and Fares and Ticketing Arrangements

There are examples of operators working together to allow ticket holders to use services run by another operator. These are currently, however, few and far between. In addition, concessionary travel (although an important part of a commercial operator's business) is also currently constrained in terms of the classes of people that can use it. There is a need for fares and ticketing arrangements which:

- are based on the objectives of both modal shift and enhanced accessibility to meet the social needs of targeted groups;
- promote cross-subsidisation of travel on routes to ensure service continuity throughout the day;
- are targeted on a route and geographical basis;
- are affordable, for targeted groups with particular needs;
- help to overcome patterns of financial exclusion.

Financial exclusion was an important issue identified by Castlemilk Economic Development Agency. Loans to assist with the purchase of motor vehicles to help with travel to work were potentially problematic in terms of the banking sector's concerns over repayments. For residents who had just started work, the agency were currently able to pay for their zone card and they would be reimbursed when the recipient had received their first pay cheque. The household survey also identified that a large proportion of bus users on low incomes tended to pay more on fares in a typical week than those on higher incomes.

Ticketing initiatives were felt to be an extremely important area of activity, but the current emphasis is clearly geared towards modal shift. There are examples of operators working together to allow season ticket holders to use services run by another operator. An inter-ticketing scheme has also been put forward by the South of Scotland Transport Partnership. The emphasis within the scheme is modal shift, although it is anticipated that it could have an impact on travel by the socially excluded. There is clearly scope within new ticketing arrangements for targeted cross-subsidisation to be discussed on a geographical or route basis.

Provision of Public Transport in New Developments

Land-use planning is regarded as extremely important not only in terms of the provision of community facilities, but also of the location of new employment and retail centres which could easily be served by public transport. Operators and the local authorities all cited the important role of land-use planning. Operators also viewed developments such as new housing schemes and new industrial estates, where bus facilities had been incorporated into the development, more favourably. Transport and planning authorities should:

- promote the role of public transport in new developments;
- provide specified facilities in discussion with operators to promote new services;
- encourage new developments to areas that are well served by public transport.

Public transport provision in new developments is essential if new developments, particularly those located at edge of town or out-of-town locations, are to be accessible to excluded groups who are more reliant on public transport. The interviews with local authorities and operators (Chapter 6) revealed instances where little thought had been put into public transport accessibility at new developments.

Provision of Cycling and Pedestrian Infrastructure

Walking was found to be a very significant mode of transport in each case study area. Further analysis revealed a strong link between local neighbourhood and mode choice. Walking accounted for a significant share of journeys within the local neighbourhood for many different trip purposes (for example, 74 per cent of journeys to the local shop). Cycling, on the other hand, accounted for less than 2 per cent of journeys to all types of activities. Cycling and walking are viewed favourably where the distances are small; they are both seen as healthy activities. In Leith and Castlemilk respondents commented on the need to move to improve their transport links and accessibility – investment in cycling and walking infrastructure will help to promote patterns of sustainable transport use. Provision of cycling and walking infrastructure will:

- protect the role that walking plays in terms of mode share in local neighbourhoods and encourage walking activity;
- enhance the status of cycling and encourage a growth in mode share;

- promote healthy lifestyles in poor neighbourhoods;
- improve accessibility and environmental quality and contribute to improved perceptions of safety.

Non-transport Solutions

This area requires further research in order fully to evaluate the potential for ICT in assisting with the provision of targeted services for particular social groups. Some work also considered the value of non-transport solutions to the pressures on time budgets. New communication technologies are often heralded as a medium designed to reduce the pressures on time use. Examples provided are the use of the Internet to access resources providing information on travel timetables and routes, allowing for better projection of time expenditure. Although new technology is potentially useful, in itself it does not resolve issues about skills and labour market demand and supply; new technology is potentially useful as it offers another avenue through which opportunities arise to organisations and individuals.

Data from this work found that 38 per cent owned a PC within the case study areas and 41 per cent stated they had access to email. Nonetheless. at this time Internet access was more likely to be found in wealthier households. Twenty-seven per cent (n=82) did feel, however, that Internet access would make a great deal of difference in terms of accessing information.

What are the Implications of the Social Exclusion Debate for the Delivery and Organisation of Transport Policy?

It has been argued, with examples, that the process of social exclusion and its relationship with transport provision is little understood by local authorities. This in itself is a serious flaw, given that local authorities, in accordance with the thrust of an integrated transport policy, are charged with developing fully accessible systems that promote seamless travel (Hine and Mitchell, 2001a; Hine and Mitchell, 2001b). Other work has indicated that local authorities in Scotland are good at specifying targets and objectives in their Local Transport Strategies but poor at analyses of the geographical distribution of local exclusion and the benefits of particular interventions into the local transport market (Sinclair et al., 2001).

Clearly, local transport strategies in Scotland as a mechanism or statement of intent in terms of the allocation of resources for dealing with transport related social exclusion, have some way to go, but they provide a benchmark and plan by which central government resources are to be used. The Transport (Scotland) Act 2001 has placed an added requirement for strategies to be in place before funding is made available. It also puts legislation in place for Quality Partnerships and Quality Contracts, integrated ticketing schemes and road pricing. The issue for the future is the degree to which these interventions can tackle exclusion at a time when the main objective of policy is to tackle car dependence and facilitate a modal shift from private to public transport. The advocacy of quality bus corridors is symptomatic of this view. For the customer of public transport, they can deliver required journey times, reliability and services at a higher frequency. One the other hand, in order for operators to deliver these services, it may mean they have to distinguish between primary routes – that is, more profitable parts of the network – and secondary routes, where older vehicles and infrastructure are in place. It is clear that urban corridors are more profitable parts of any network.

Earlier in this chapter particular policy interventions and the way in which they could impact on transport related social exclusion were discussed. It has been pointed out that socially excluded groups are not only found clustered in particular areas; they can also be found in scatters as a consequence of life circumstance (Grieco, Turner and Hine, 2000). This represents a fundamentally different problem for policy makers than a cluster. It has been argued that the scatter of socially excluded individuals and households can be better served through new information technologies where reservations systems can be used for demand responsive transport. For clusters of the socially excluded, it may be relatively easier to provide services and they may offer a better fit with existing bus routes and schedules. That is not say to that clusters are not without their problems. In circumstances where subsidised services are offered at particular times of the day to help people access job opportunities in other areas, the services may be well used initially but then operators experience a decline in patronage as these passengers become more established in the work force and begin to be able to share transport with colleagues or even, over a period of time, purchase a car.

Annex

Methodology

Questionnaire Design

The questionnaire survey was developed from existing questionnaires used to gather data on travel patterns and from the Scottish Household Survey. Some qualitative work was also undertaken to help inform the design of the questions and structure of the survey instrument. The final questionnaire was designed around a number of key areas:

- housing;
- health;
- labour markets and employment;
- education;
- income and welfare;
- social networks;
- neighbourhoods;
- transport, including car access, driving, public transport, taxis, walking and cycling.

Importantly, the design of the questionnaire allowed transport choices and limitations to be placed in the wider context of health, education, household structure, age and gender, and household income.

Survey Method

The household survey was undertaken in three case study areas: Leith, Coatbridge and Castlemilk. The specific locality for each survey area was the electoral ward for each area. For Leith this was Harbour ward, in Castlemilk it was the Castlemilk ward itself, and for Coatbridge the wards of Kirkshaws and Old Monklands were used. Age/sex profiles for each area were generated from the census small area statistics for each area so that a framework for obtaining a quota sample could be obtained.

The objective was to contact a quota of 200 people in each area, reflecting the age, sex and car ownership characteristics of the resident populations in each of these areas. The total sample sizes for each area at the end of the data collection stage were 189 for Leith, Harbour; 180 for Castlemilk and 183 for Kirkshaws and Old Monkland, Coatbridge. In line with the objectives of the study, a significant proportion of the sample were found to own no car.

In-depth Interviews

In-depth interview data were used to form the basis of Chapter 6. Fifteen such interviews with representatives of the bus industry and local authorities in each area responsible for services and strategywere conducted for this phase of the project . All the interviews were tape-recorded and transcribed. A subject guide was used to prompt the interviewer to cover all salient issues but also to allow flexibility so that points raised within the interview could be explored.

Table A1   Bus service frequencies in the case study areas – local bus services in Leith

Service	Frequency (every stated time in minutes)		
	Monday–Friday	Saturday	Sunday
35/35A – Lothian Buses	10–15 day 30 after 1941hrs	30 early am 15–20 day 30 after 1744hrs	30 all day
1 – Lothian Buses	15 day 30 after 1830hrs	15 day 30 after 1900hrs	30 all day
2 – Lothian Buses	30 early am 20 day 30 after 2145hrs	30	30 all day
12 – Lothian Buses	10–20 early am 10 all day 30 after 2000hrs	30 early am 10 all day 30 after 2112hrs	30 all day
10/10A – Lothian Buses	10–20 early am 12 all day 30 after 1842hrs	30 early am 15 all day 30 after 1816hrs	30 all day
14/14B – Lothian Buses	20–30 all day 30 after 1945hrs	30 early am 15–20 all day 30 after 1945hrs	30 all day
16 – Lothian Buses	20–30 early am	15–20 all day 30 after 1900hrs	30 all day
17 – Lothian Buses	20 early am 15 all day	15 all day	15–30 all day

Table A1 cont'd

Service	Frequency (every stated time in minutes)		
	Monday–Friday	Saturday	Sunday
22 – Lothian Buses	15 early am 10–15 all day	15 early am 10 all day 15 after 1922hrs	15 all day
25/25A – Lothian Buses	10 early am 10 all day 30 after 1857hrs	20 all day 30 after 1830hrs	30 all day
34 – Lothian Buses	20 all day 30 after 1923hrs	20 all day 10 after 1823hrs	30 all day
7 – Lothian Buses	20 all day 30 after 1918hrs	20 all day 30 after 1918 hrs	30 all day

Table A2   Bus service frequencies in the case study areas – local bus services in Castlemilk

Service	Frequency (every stated time in minutes)		
	Monday–Friday	*Saturday*	*Sunday*
5 (FIRST)	10 all day 20 after 1750 hrs	60 early am 10–20 all day 20 after 1847hrs	15 all day 20 after 1741 hrs
31 (FIRST)	30 all day	30 all day	1 hour
32 (FIRST)	30 all day	30 all day	No service
34 (FIRST)	30 early am 15 day 30 after 1740hrs	30 early am 15 all day 30 after 1720 hrs	30 am 15 all day 30 after 1700 hrs
37 (FIRST)	15 all day 30 after 1740hrs	30 early am 15 all day 30 after 1720hrs	30 am 15 all day 30 after 1700hrs
46 (FIRST)	30 early am 20 all day 30 after 1900hrs	20 all day 30 after 1825hrs	30 all day
74 (FIRST)	15–30 all day	20 all day 30 after 1835hrs	30 all day
75 (FIRST)	10 all day 20 after 1717hrs	10 all day 20 after 2225 hrs	10 all day 20 after 2225 hrs
95 (FIRST/DART)	30 all day	30 all day	No service
95 (DART)	30 all day	30 all day	No service
134 (First Stop Travel)	No timetable information		
234 (First Stop Travel)	No timetable information		

Table A3   Bus service frequencies in the case study areas – local bus services in Coatbridge

Service	Frequency (every stated time in minutes)		
	Monday–Friday	Saturday	Sunday
5201 (FIRST)	30 early am	30 early am	30 all day
	10 all day	10 all day	
	30 after 1856hrs	30 after 1842hrs	
260 (Coakley)	30 all day	30 all day	1 hour
SO2 (VALEW Tours)	1 hour	No service	No service
X1 Bruces Coaches	One return service leaving		
	Shotts at 0720	No service	No service

Bibliography

Abdalla, I., Raeside, R., Barker, D.J. and McQuigan, D.R. (1997), 'An Investigation into the Relationships between Area Social Characteristics and Road Accident Casualties', *Accident Analysis and Prevention*, Vol. 29, No. 5.

Abt Associates Inc. (1969), *Transportation Needs of the Handicapped: Travel Barriers*, Abt Associates Inc., Cambridge, MA.

Anon (n.d.) *Interconnecting Digital Communities (InterCom)*. *Devon, UK*, available online at http://www.eltis.org/data/116e.htm.

Arnott, R. (1998), 'Economic theory and the spatial mismatch hypothesis', *Urban Studies*, Vol. 35, No. 7, pp. 1171–1185.

Atkins, S. (1989), 'Women, Travel and Personal Security', in Grieco, M., Pickup, L. and Whipp, R. (1989), *Gender, Transport and Employment: The impact of travel constraints*, Gower, Aldershot.

Atkinson, A.B. and Hills, J. (eds) (1998), *Exclusion, Employment and Opportunity*, London School of Economics and Political Science, Centre for Analysis of Social Exclusion, London.

Audit Commission (1999), *A Life's Work: Local authorities, economic development and economic regeneration*, HMSO, London.

Backett, E.M. and Johnston, A.M. (1959), 'Social Patterns of Road Accidents to Children: Some characteristics of vulnerable families', *British Medical Journal*, 1, pp. 409–13.

Balcombe, R.J. and Finch, D.J. (1990), *Shared Taxi Schemes in Britain. Lessons Learnt in Ipswich*, Research Report 292, Transport and Road Research Laboratory, Crowthorne.

Barry, B. (1998), *Social Exclusion, Social Isolation and the Distribution of Income*, Centre for Analysis of Social Exclusion, London School of Economics, London.

Beuret, K. (1994), 'Taxis: The neglected mode in public transport planning', in *Provision for Accessible Transport Services*, Proceedings of Seminar F held at the PTRC European Transport Forum, London.

Beuret, K. (1995), 'Call a Cab – Chance would be a Fine Thing: The importance of taxi transport for elderly and disabled people and the problems of provision', *Proceedings of 7th International Conference Mobility and Transport for Elderly and Disabled People*, Reading, 16–19 July, pp. 317–22.

Bhalla, A. and Lapeyre, F. (1997), 'Social Exclusion: Towards an analytical and operational framework', *Development and Change*, Vol. 28, No. 3, pp. 413–33.

Blake Stevenson Ltd (1994), *Evaluation of Castlemilk to East Kilbride Pilot Bus Link Project*, Castlemilk Economic Development Agency (CEDA) and Glasgow Development Agency.

Bly, P. (1993), 'Growing Older, Wish to Travel', in Clayton, A (ed.), *Older Road Users: The role of government and the professions*, AA Foundation for Road Safety Research, Basingstoke.

Bonsall, P. and Dunkerley, C. (1997) 'Use of Concessionary Travel Permits in London: Results of a diary survey', *Public Transport Planning and Operations*, Proceedings of Seminar G held at the PTRC European Transport Forum, London.

Borjesson, M. (1989), *Public Transport for Everyone*, TFB Report 1989:1, Swedish Transport Research Board, Stockholm.

Brennan, A., Rhodes, J., and Tyler, P. (1998), *New Findings on the Nature of Economic and Social Exclusion in England and the Implications for New Policy Initiative*, Department of Land Economy, University of Cambridge, Cambridge.

Brooks, B.M., Ruffell-Smith, H.P. and Ward, J.S. (1974), *An Investigation of Factors Affecting the use of Buses by both Elderly and Ambulant Disabled Persons*, British Leyland UK Ltd (Truck and Bus Division), Leyland.

Burchardt, T., Le Grand, J. and Piachaud, D. (1999), 'Social Exclusion in Britain 1991–1995', *Social Policy and Administration*, Vol. 33, No. 3, pp. 227–44.

Burkett, N. (2000), *Own Transport Preferred: Transport and social exclusion in North East*, Low Pay Unit, Newcastle.

Byrne, A. and Holt, A. (1995), 'Positioning the User at the Centre of the Public Transport Planning and Provision Framework', *Proceedings of 7th International Conference on Mobility and Transport for Elderly and Disabled People*, Vol. 1, pp. 115–22.

Callender, C. (1999), *The Hardship of Learning: Students' income and expenditure and their impact on participation in further education*, The Further Education Funding Council.

Carter, C. and Grieco, M. (1998), 'New Deals, No Wheels: Social exclusion, teleology and electronic ontology', *Urban Studies*, Vol. 37, No. 10.

Chamberlayne, P. (1996), *Social Exclusion in Comparative Perspective: SOSTRIS Working Paper 1*, Centre for Biography in Social Policy, University of East London, Dagenham.

Church, A. and Frost, M. (1999), *Transport and Social Exclusion in London: Exploring current and potential indicators*, London Transport Planning, London.

Church, A., Frost, M. and Sullivan, K. (2000) *Transport and Social Exclusion in London – Report Summary*, London Transport Planning, London.

Church, A., Frost, M. and Sullivan, K. (2001), 'Transport and Social Exclusion in London', *Journal of Transport Policy*, Vol. 7, No. 3, pp. 195–205.

City of Edinburgh Council (2001), *Local Transport Strategy 2000–2004*, City of Edinburgh Council.

Cloke, P., Milbourne, P. and Thomas, C. (1997), 'Living Life in Different Ways? Deprivation, Marginalization and Changing Lifestyles in Rural England', *Transactions of the Institute of British Geographers*, Vol. 22 (2), pp. 210–30 .

Cohen, P. (1996), 'Greying Population stays in the Pink', *New Scientist*, Vol. 151, No. 2021, p. 4.

Crime Concern and Transport and Travel Research (1997), *Perceptions of Safety from Crime on Public Transport*, Department of Transport, London.

Crime Concern (1999a) *Personal Security Issues in Pedestrian Journeys*, Department of Environment, Transport and the Regions, London.

Crime Concern (1999b) *Young People and Crime on Public Transport*, Department of Environment, Transport and the Regions, London.

Dasgupta, M. (1982a), *Mobility and Access to Employment Opportunities: A Comparison of Inner and Outer Areas of Greater Manchester*, TRRL Laboratory Report LR1054, Transport and Road Research Laboratory, Crowthorne.

Dasgupta, M. (1982b), *Access to Employment Opportunities by Car and by Bus in Inner and Outer Areas of Manchester*, TRRL Supplementary Report SR 741, Transport and Road Research Laboratory, Crowthorne.

Dasgupta, M. (1983), *Employment and Work Travel in an Inner Area Context*, TRRL Supplementary Report SR 780, Transport and Road Research Laboratory, Crowthorne.

De Monchaux, S. (1981), *Planning with Children in Mind: A notebook for local planners and policy makers on children in the city environment*, NSW Department of Environment and Planning, Sydney.

DfEE (1998), *New Arrangements for Effective Student Support in Further Education*, Report of the Further Education Student Support Advisory Group, London.

DfEE (1999), *Jobs for All, Report of the Policy Action Team on Jobs for the National Strategy for Neighbourhood Renewal*, London.

DETR (1998a), *A New Deal for Transport: Better for everyone, the government's White Paper on the future of transport*, Cm3950, HMSO, London.

DETR (1998b), *Focus on Personal Travel*, TSO, London.

DETR (1999a) *Low Floor Bus Trials in a Rural Area*, available online at http://www.mobility-unit.detr.gov.uk/lowfloor/execsum.htm

DETR (1999b) *Review of Voluntary Transport*, available online at http://www.mobility-unit.detr.gov.uk/rvt/report/1.htm

DETR (1999c), *Young People and Crime on Public Transport*, DETR, London.

DETR (2000a), *Social Exclusion and the Provision and Availability of Public Transport*, DETR, London.

DETR (2000b), *A Review of the Evidence Base for Regeneration Policy and Practice*, London.

DETR (2001), *Older People: Their transport needs and requirements*, London.

DLTR (2001), *Urban Bus Challenge 2002: Guidance on criteria and arrangements*, London.

Donald, R.G. and Pickup, L. (1991), 'The Effects of Local Bus Deregulation in Great Britain on Low Income Families: The case of Merseyside', *Transportation Planning and Technology*, Vol. 15 (2/4), pp. 331–47.

Duguid, G. (1995), *Deprived Areas in Scotland: Results of an analysis of the 1991 Census*, Central Research Unit, Edinburgh.

ECMT (1986), *Transport for Disabled People: International comparisons of practices and policies with recommendations for change*, European Conference of Ministers of Transport, Paris.

Elliot, B. (1985), *Children and Road Accidents: An analysis of the problems and some suggested solutions*, Federal Office of Road Safety, Road Safety Report CR36, Department of Transport, Canberra.

Engwicht, D. (1992), *Towards an Eco-city: Calming the traffic*, Envirobook, Sydney.

Evans, D.S. and Smyth, A.W. (1997), 'Fully Scheduled or Dial-a-ride? The Future Direction of Accessibility Policy for Local Public Transport', *Public Transport Planning and Operations. Proceedings of Seminar G*, PTRC European Transport Forum, London.

Farrington, J., Gray, D., Martin, S. and Roberts, D. (1998), *Car Dependence in Rural Scotland: Challenges and policies*, Central Research Unit, Scottish Office, Edinburgh.

Federal Transit Administration (FTA) (1999), *Welfare-to Work (Job Access and Reverse Community Initiative*, available online at http://www.fta.dot.gov/wtw.

Flores, J.-L., Bonnardel, G. and Pachiaudi, G. (1981), *Confort dans l'autobus – approche ergonomique*. IRT Note d'information No. 19, Institute de Recherche des Transports, Arcueil.

Folwell, K. (1999), *Getting the Measure of Social Exclusion*, London Research Centre, Demographic and Statistical Studies, London.

Fowkes, A., Smoczynski, J. and Watkins, I. (1987), *A Study of the Ergonomics of Minibuses for Disabled and Elderly People*, MIRA Report K48575, Motor Industry Research Association, Nuneaton.

Gaerling, T., Gillholm, R. and Montgomery, W. (1998), 'Computer Simulations of Consequences of Time Pressure for Activity/Travel Choices', World Conference of Transport Research, Antwerp, Belgium, July.

Gaffron, P., Hine, J. and Mitchell, F. (2001), *The Role of Transport in Social Exclusion in Urban Scotland: Literature review*, Scottish Executive Central Research Unit, Edinburgh.

Gallon, C., Fowkes, A. and Edwards, M. (1995), *Accidents involving Visually Impaired People using Public Transport or Walking*, TRL Project PR 82, Transport Research Laboratory, Crowthorne.

Gibb, K., Kearns, A., Keoghan, M., MacKay, D. and Turok, I. (1998), *Revising the Scottish Area Deprivation Index (Vol. 1)*, Central Research Unit, Scottish Office, Edinburgh.

GLAD (1986), *All Change: A consumer study of public transport handicap in London*, Greater London Association for Disabled People, London.

Glennerster, H. (1999), *Poverty, Social Exclusion and Neighbourhood: Studying the area bases of social exclusion*, Centre for Analysis of Social Exclusion, London School of Economics, London.

Gorter, C., Nijkamp, P. and Rietveld, P. (1993), 'Barriers to Employment – Entry and Reentry Possibilities of Unemployed Job Seekers in the Netherlands', *Economist*, Vol. 141, No. 1, pp. 70–95.

Grayling, T. (2001), 'Transport and Social Exclusion', paper presented to the Transport Statistics User Group, January.

Greater Manchester PTE (n.d.), *Bus Service Improvement in Salford City Counci*, available online at http://194.7.159.227/GEDdata/1999/10/13/00000001/1310991d.htm

Green, A.E. (1995), 'The Changing Structure, Distribution and Spatial Segregation of the Unemployed and Economically Inactive in Great Britain', *Geoforum*, Vol. 26, No. 4, pp. 373–94.

Green, A.E. (1998), *Social Exclusion, the Journey to Work and Ethnic Minorities* (overheads of a presentation for a workshop on Social Exclusion and Transport at the University of Manchester on 26 November), available online at http://www.art.man.ac.uk/transres/socexclu1.htm

Grieco, M., Pickup, L. and Whipp, R. (1989), *Gender, Transport and Employment*, Gower, Aldershot.

Grieco, M., Turner, J. and Hine, J. (2000), 'Transport, Employment and Social Exclusion', *Local Work*, 26.

Grieco, M. and Turner, J. (1997), 'Gender, Poverty and Transport: A call for policy action', address delivered at UN International Forum on Urban Poverty, Florence.

GROS (1997), *Mid Year Population Estimates*, GRO, Edinburgh.

Guidez, J.M. (1994), 'Urban Transport and Exclusion in Public Transport', *Planning and Operation: Procceedings of Seminar E*, 22nd PTRC European Transport Forum, London.

De Haan, A. (1999), *Social Exclusion: Towards an holistic understanding of deprivation*, Department for International Development, London.

Hamilton, K., Hoyle, S.R. and Jenkins, L. (2000), *The Public Transport Gender Audit*, TSO, London

Hamilton, K. and Jenkins, L. (1992), 'Women and Transport', in Roberts, J et al. (eds), *Travel Sickness*, Lawrence and Wishart, London.

Hamilton, K., Jenkins, L. and Gregory, A. (1991), *Women and Transport: Bus deregulation in West Yorkshire*, University of Bradford, Bradford.

Hanlon, S. (1996), *Where do Women Feature in Public Transport?*, US Department of Transportation, Federal Highway Administration, Washington.

Harbert, W. (1994), 'Taxis. Are Infirm and Frail People being Left Behind? The Case for Swivel Seats', in *Provision for Accessible Transport Services*, proceedings of Seminar F held at the PTRC European Transport Forum, PTRC Education and Research services Ltd, London.

Harman, L.J and Thatcher, R.H. (1995), 'Accessible Transit Options for Persons with Disabilities – the United States Approach', *Proceedings of 7th International Conference Mobility and Transport for Elderly and Disabled People*, Reading, 16–19 July, pp. 210–17.

Harris, A.I. (1971), *Handicapped and Impaired in Great Britain, Part 1*, HMSO, London.

Herbert, S. (1996), *New Ideas in Rural Development No 2: Action on Scottish Rural Transport – Helping Local Communities Tackle their Transport Problems*, Central Research Unit, The Scottish Office, Edinburgh.

Hillman, M. and Whalley, A. (1979), *Walking is Transport*, Policy Studies Institute, London.

Hillman, M., Adams, J. and Whitelegg, J. (1990), *One False Move ... A Study of Children's Independent Mobility*, PSI, London.

Hine, J.P. and Mitchell, F. (2001a), *The Role of Public Transport in Social Exclusion*, Scottish Executive Central Research Unit, Edinburgh.

Hine, J.P. and Mitchell, F. (2001b), 'Better for Everyone? Travel Experiences and Transport Exclusion', *Urban Studies*, Vol. 38, pp. 319–32.

Hine, J. and Scott, J. (2001), 'Seamless, Accessible Travel: Users' views of the public transport journey and interchange', *Journal of Transport Policy*, Vol. 7, No. 3, pp. 217–26.

Hitchcock, A. and Mitchell, C.G.B. (1984), 'Man and his Walking Behaviour. Part a. Walking as a Means of Transport', *Transport Reviews*, Vol. 4, No. 2, pp. 177–87.

Holzer, H.J, Ihlanfeldt, K.R. and Sjoquist, D.L. (1994), 'Work, Search and Travel among White and Black Youth', *Journal of Urban Economics*, Vol. 35, No. 3, pp. 320–45.

Hopkin, J. and Oxley, P. (1989), *The Effects of Bus Service Reduction in Urban Areas: Case studies in Oxford and Manchester*, Transport and Road Research Laboratory, Crowthorne.

Hopkin, J., Robson, P. and Town, S.W. (1978), *The Mobility of Old People: A study in Guildford*, TRRL Laboratory Report LR850, Transport and Road Research Laboratory, Crowthorne.

House of Commons (1999), *Poverty and Social Exclusion (National Strategy) Bill* (as presented to the House of Commons on 10 February), available online at http://www.parliament.the-stationery-office.co.uk/ pa/cm199899/cmbills/045/ 1999045.htm.

Kegerris, S. (1993), 'Independent Mobility and Children's Mental and Emotional Development', in Hillman, M. (ed.), *Children, Transport and the Quality of Life*, Policy Studies Institute, London.

Kleinman, M. (1998), *Include me Out: The new politics of place and poverty*, Centre for Analysis of Social Exclusion, London School of Economics, London.

Lawless, P. (1995), 'Inner-city and Suburban Labour Markets in a Major English Conurbation – Processes and Policy Implications', *Urban Studies*, Vol. 32, No. 7, pp. 1097–125.

Lawson, S.D. and Edwards, P.J. (1991), 'The Involvement of Ethnic Minorities in Road Accidents: Data from three studies of young pedestrian casualties', *Traffic Engineering and Control*, January, pp. 12–19.

Lavery, I, Davey, S. and McKenna, O. (1992), 'Transport Deprivation and Marginalisation of People with a Mobility Handicap in Northern Ireland', *Transport for People with a Mobility Handicap*,proceedings of Seminar F at PTRC 20 Summer Annual Meeting, London.

Leake, G.R., May, A.D. and Parry, T. (1991), *An Ergonomic Study of Pedestrian Areas for Disabled People*, Contractor Report CR 184, Transport and Road Research Laboratory, Crowthorne.

Lee, P. and Murie, A. (1999), *Literature Review of Social Exclusion,* Central Research Unit, Edinburgh.

Levinson, D.M. and Kumar, A. (1994), 'The Rational Locator – Why Travel Times have Remained Stable', *Journal of the American Planning Association*, Vol. 60, No. 3, pp. 319–32.

Leyshon, A. and Thrift, N. (1995), 'Geographies of Financial Exclusion: Financial abandonment in Britain and the United States', *Transactions of the Institute of British Geographers*, Vol. 20, No. 3, pp. 312–41.

Ling, D.J. and Mannion, R. (1995), 'Improving Older People's Mobility and Quality of Life: An assessment of the economic and social benefits of dial-a-ride', *Proceedings of 7th International Conference Mobility and Transport for Elderly and Disabled People*, Reading, 16–19 July, pp. 331–9.

Littlewood, P. and Herkammer, S. (1999), 'Identifying Social Exclusion. Some Problems of Meaning', in Littlewood, P. (ed.), *Social Exclusion in Europe: Problems and paradigms*, Ashgate Publishing Ltd, Aldershot.

Lucas, K., Grosvenor, T. and Simpson, R. (2001), *Transport, the Environment and Social Exclusion*, York Publishing Services, York.

MacKenzie, I. (1993), 'The Evolution of "Specialised Schemes" and their Contribution towards the Provision of Needs-based Integrated Accessible Passenger Transport Services', *Transport for People with a Mobility Handicap*, Proceedings of Seminar J, held at the PTRC Transport, Highways and Planning Summer Annual Meeting. London.

Martin, J., Meltzer, H. and Eliot, D. (1988), *OPCS Surveys of Disability in Great Britain: Report 1 The Prevalence of Disability among Adults*, Office of Population Census and Surveys, HMSO, London.

Martin, J., White, A. and Meltzer, H. (1988), *OPCS Surveys of Disability in Great Britain: Report 4 Disabled Adults: Services, Transport and Employment*, Office of Population Census and Surveys, HMSO, London.

McCormick, J.and Leicester, G. (1998), *Three Nations. Social Exclusion in Scotland*, available online at http://www.scottishpolicynet.org.uk/scf/publications/paper_3/frameset.shtml.

McGregor, A., Fitzpatrick, I. and Glass, A. (1998), *Regeneration Areas and Barriers to Employment*, Central Research Unit, Edinburgh.

McGregor, A. and McConnachie, M. (1995), 'Social Exclusion, Urban Regeneration and Economic Reintegration', *Urban Studies*, Vol. 32, No. 10, pp. 1587–600.

McKee, C. (1993), 'Making Rail Vehicles accessible to Disabled Passengers', *Transport for People with a Mobility Handicap*, Proceedings of Seminar J, PTRC Transport, Highways and Planning Summer Annual Meeting, London.

McLary, M. (1995), 'The Role of Taxis in Accessible Transport', *Proceedings of 7th International Conference Mobility and Transport for Elderly and Disabled People*, Reading, 16–19 July, pp. 307–16.

Mensah, J. (1995), 'Journey to Work and Job Search Characteristics of the Urban Poor – A Gender Analysis of Survey Data from Edmonton, Alberta', *Transportation*, Vol. 22, No. 1, pp. 1–19.

MerseyTravel (1998) *Community Links Strategy*, MerseyTravel, Liverpool.

Mitchell, C.G.B. (1988), *Features on Buses to Assist Passengers with Mobility Handicaps*, TRRL Research Report RR137, Transport and Road Research Laboratory, Crowthorne.

Mitchell, C.G.B. (1997), *Access to Transport Systems and Services: An international review*, Transportation Development Centre, Transport Canada.

Monk, S., Dunn, J., Fitzgerald, M. and Hodge, I. (1999), *Finding Work in Rural Areas: Barriers and bridges*, York Publishing Services, York.

Moseley, M.J. (1979), *Accessibility: The rural challenge*, London: Methuen

National Consumer Council (1987), *What's Wrong with Walking?*, National Consumer Council, HMSO, London.

Newsom, T.J., Petty, D.M. and Henderson, C. (1993), 'Transportation Service Demonstrations to Facilitate the Employment of Persons with Disabilities', *Transportation Research Record* (1378), pp. 10–15

Office of National Statistics (1998), *Social Focus on Women and Men*, TSO, London.

Olshansky, S.J., Carnes, B.A. and Cassess, C.K. (1993), 'The Aging of the Human Species', *Scientific American*, April, pp. 18–24.

Oxley, P.R. (1977), 'Dial a Ride in the UK: A general study', in TRRL (eds), *Symposium on Unconventional Bus Services*, WP 23, Transport and Road Research Laboratory, Crowthorne.

Oxley, P.R and Alexander, J. (1994), *Disability and Mobility in London – A Follow Up to the London Area Travel Survey*, TRL PR34, Transport Research Laboratory, Crowthorne.

Oxley, P.R. and Benwell, M. (1985), *An Experimental Study of the Use of Buses by Elderly and Disabled People*, TRRL Research Report RR33, Transport and Road Research Laboratory, Crowthorne.

O'Connor, W. and Lewis, J. (1999), *Experiences of Social Exclusion in Scotland. A Qualitative Research Study*, Edinburgh: Central Research Unit.

O'Regan, K.M. and Quigley, J.M. (1998), 'Where Youth Lives: Economic effects of urban space on employment prospects', *Urban Studies*, Vol. 35, No. 7, pp. 1187–205.

O'Reilly, D.M. (1989), *Concessionary Fares and Children's Travel Patterns: An analysis based on the 1978/1979 National Travel Survey*, Department of Transport, (Research Report 203), London.

O'Reilly, D.M (1990), *An Analysis of Concessionary Bus Fare Schemes for OAPs using the 1985/86 National Travel Survey*, Department of Transport (Research Report 291), London.

Pacione, M. (1995), 'The Geography of Deprivation in Rural Scotland', *Transactions of the Institute of British Geographers*, Vol. 20, No 2, pp. 173–92.

Pain, R.H. (1997), 'Social Geography of Women's Fear of Crime', *Transactions of the Institute of British Geographers*, Vol. 22, No. 2, pp. 231–44.

Perrett, K., Hopkin, J., Pickett, M. and Walmsley, D. (1989), *The Effect of Bus Deregulation in the Metropolitan Areas*, Transport and Road Research Laboratory, Crowthorne.

Pickup, L. (1989), 'Women's Travel Requirements: Employment, with domestic constraints', in Grieco, M., Pickup, L. and Whipp, R, (1989), *Gender, Transport and Employment: The impact of travel constraints*, Gower, Aldershot.

Polk, M. (1996), *Swedish Men and Women's Mobility Patterns: Issues of social equity and ecological sustainability*, US Department of Transportation, Federal Highway Administration, Washington DC.

Preston, B. (1972), 'Statistical Analysis of Child Pedestrian Accidents in Manchester and Salford', *Accident Analysis and Prevention*, 4, pp. 323–32.

Read, J.H., Bradley, E.J., Morison, J.D., Lewall, D. and Clarke, D.A. (1963), 'The Epidemiology and Prevention of Traffic Accidents involving Child Pedestrians', *Canadian Medical Association Journal*, 89, pp. 687–701.

Reid-Howie Associates (2000), *Women and Transport: Moving forward*, Scottish Executive Central Research Unit, Edinburgh.

Rosenbloom, S. (1989), 'Trip Chaining Behaviour', in Grieco, M., Pickup, L. and Whipp, R, (1989), *Gender, Transport and Employment: The impact of travel constraints*, Gower, Aldershot.

Rosenbloom, S. (1992), 'Mobility: Indicator or determinant of aging and impairment?', *Proceedings of the 6th International Conference on Mobility and Transport for Elderly and Disabled Persons*, Lyon.

Rosenbloom, S. (1996), *Trends in Women's Travel Patterns*, US Department of Transportation, Federal Highway Administration, Washington DC.

Royal Commission on Environmental Pollution (1994), *Transport and the Environment*, Oxford University Press, Oxford.

Rural Development Commission (1999), *Labour Market Detachment in Rural England*, Rural Research Report No. 40.

SAMPLUS (1999), *SAMPLUS: Demand Responsive Transport*, available online at http://www. Europrojects.ie/samplusmainweb.

SAPT (1998), *Access and Social Inclusion: A response to the Scottish Office Consultation paper on social exclusion*, Scottish Association for Public Transport, Glasgow.

Scottish Executive (2001), *Scottish Household Survey*, Scottish Executive, Edinburgh.

Scottish Office Education and Industry Department (SOEID) (1998), *Widening Participation in Higher Education: Report of National Conference at Glasgow Caledonian University*, The Scottish Office, Edinburgh.

Scottish Social Inclusion Network (1998), *Social Inclusion Draft Strategy*, available online at http://www.scotland.gov.uk/inclusion/ssin10anx.htm.

Scottish Social Inclusion Strategy Action Team (1999), *Inclusive Communities*, Social Inclusion Division, Scottish Executive, Edinburgh.

Select Committee on Education and Employment (1998), *Education and Employment –7th report: Overcoming barriers to paid employment for lone parents*, available on line at http://www.parliament.the-stationery-office.co.uk/pa/cm199798/cmselect/cmeduemp/646/64602.htm.

Sinclair, S.P. (2001), *Financial Exclusion: An introductory survey*, Centre for Research into Socially Inclusive Services (CRSIS), Edinburgh College of Art/Heriot-Watt University.

Sinclair, S.P and Sinclair, F. (2001), *Access all Areas? An Assessment of Social Inclusion Measures in Scottish Local Transport Strategies*, Centre for Research into Socially Inclusive Services (CRSIS), Edinburgh College of Art/Heriot-Watt University.

Smith, G.R. (1999), *Area-based Initiatives: The rationale and options for area targeting*, Centre for Analysis of Social Exclusion, London School of Economics, London.

Social Exclusion Unit (1998), *Bringing Britain Together: A national strategy for neighbourhood renewal*, Cabinet Office, London.

Social Exclusion Unit (2001), *National Strategy for Neighbourhood Renewal: Policy Action Team Audit*, Cabinet Office, London.

Somerville, P. (1998), 'Explanations of Social Exclusion: Where does housing fit in?', *Housing Studies*, Vol. 13, No. 6, pp. 761–80.

Speller, B.E. and Mitchell, C.G.B. (1975), *The Harlow Dial-a-Bus Experiment* (Supplementary Report 127UC), Department of the Environment, London.

Spicker, P. (1998), *Housing and Social Exclusion: A discussion paper*, Shelter Scotland, Edinburgh.

Stafford, B., Heaver, C., Ashworth, K., Bates, C., Walker, R., McKay, S. and Trickey, H. (1999), *Young Men's Experience of the Labour Market*, Joseph Rowntree Foundation, York.

Stahl, A. (1992), 'The Provision of a Community Responsive Public Transportation in Urban Areas', *Proceedings of 6th International Conference Mobility and Transport for Elderly and Disabled People*, Lyon, 31 May– 3 June, pp. 160–67.

Stahl, A. and Brundell-Freij, K. (1995), 'The Adaptation of the Swedish Public Transport System Yesterday, Today, Tomorrow – An Evaluation', *Proceedings of 7th International Conference Mobility and Transport for Elderly and Disabled People*, Reading, 16–19 July, pp. 23–34.

System 3 (1998), *Travel Patterns in Scotland 1997: Results of an analysis of travel diaries*, Central Research Unit, Scottish Office, Edinburgh.

Systems Approach Consultants Ltd (1979), *Database Study for the Identification and Quantification of Transportation for Handicapped people in Canada*, Transport Canada Report TP 2084, Canadian Surface Transportation Administration, Transport Canada, Ottawa.

TAS Partnership (1995), *Public Transport Development in Castlemilk: Summary report*, TAS Partnership, Preston.

Taylor, J. (1993), '*Co-ordination of Accessible Transport Services,* in Transport for People with a Mobility Handicap', *Proceedings of Seminar J held at the PTRC Transport*, Highways and Planning Summer Annual Meeting, London.

Tranter, P. (1996), 'Children's Independent Mobility and Urban Form in Australasian, English and German Cities', *Proceedings of 7th World Annual Conference on Transport Research, Vol. 3 Transport Policy*, pp. 21–44, Pergamon Press.

Trench, S. and Lister, A. (1994), 'Changes in Taxi Services – Can New Developments Help People with a Mobility Handicap?', *Public Transport Planning and Operations, Proceedings of Seminar D*, held at the PTRC Transport and Planning Annual Meeting, London.

Turner, J. and Grieco, M. (1998), 'Gender, Transport and the New Deal: The social policy implications of gendered time, transport and travel', Presented at the Social Policy Association conference, Lincoln, July.

Tyrell, H. (2000), *Going My Way: What children and young people say about transport*, Save the Children, Edinburgh.

Tyson, W.J. (1995), 'Cost Effectiveness Approaches to Improving Mobility in Urban Areas', *Proceedings of 7th International Conference Mobility and Transport for Elderly and Disabled People*, Reading, 16–19 July, pp. 193–201.

United Nations (1998), *Human Development Report: Changing today's consumption patterns – for tomorrow's human development*, United Nations Development Programme.

United States Department of Transportation (1978), *Technical Report of the National Survey of Transportation Handicapped People*, Urban Mass Transit Administration, Washington DC.

United States Department of Transportation (1999), *Transport Equity Act*, available online at http://www.fhwa.dot.gov/tea21/pubs.htm.

Van Vliet, W. (1983), 'Childrens Travel Behaviour', *Ekistics*, 298, pp. 61–5.

Vidler, G. and Curtis, S. (1999), *Measuring Social Exclusion*, The Scottish Parliament Information Centre, Research Paper 99/11, Edinburgh.

York, I.O. and Balcombe, R.J. (1997), 'Accessible Bus Services: UK demonstrations', *Public Transport Planning and Operations. Proceedings of Seminar G*, European Transport Forum Annual Meeting, London.

Young, R. (1999), 'Prioritising Family Health Needs: A time-space analysis of women's health-related behaviours', *Social Science and Medicine*, Vol. 48, No. 6, pp. 797–813.

Zhang, J. and Dickson, C. (2000), 'Evaluation of the Phase Two JOBLINK Demonstration Projects: Connecting Welfare Recipients to Employment', paper presented at Annual Conference of Royal Geographical Society, University of Sussex, January.

Index